SQUASH

SQUASH

WARD LOCK

DAVID PEARSON ·

First published in 1990 by Ward Lock
Villiers House
41/47 Strand
London WC2N 5JE,
England

A Cassell imprint

Text set in 10/11pt Compugraphic Triumvirate
by BP Integraphics, Bath, Avon
Printed and bound in Great Britain
by Richard Clay Ltd, Bungay, Suffolk

ISBN 0–7063–6854–1

The Author and Publishers would like to thank
Colorsport for providing all photographs.

Frontispiece: One of the greatest players
of all time, Jansher Khan, perfectly
poised after the cross-court backhand.

CONTENTS

INTRODUCTION

It was with great pleasure that I accepted the invitation to write *Ahead of the Game: Squash.* Over the past 13 years I have combined competitive squash with coaching at the highest level and have been coaching with National squads. Furthermore, I have been fortunate enough to be selected for England 40 times in various championships and have played squash all over the world. Through this book, I intend to pass on my experience in a simple and straightforward manner.

Ahead of the Game is aimed at the more advanced player, *i.e.* the club player. The book will deal with all aspects of the game from first principles to the more advanced attacking shots. There are also sections on fitness and injury prevention which are important areas in any sport, not only squash. The reader will soon realize that squash is an easy sport to play, but it is one that requires practice and dedication in order to attain a higher standard of play.

There are comments within the book from the world's top players on their favourite shots, and why they play these shots. The section is intended to give you an insight into the thoughts of the top players, so spurring you on to greater things.

Squash is now being played by children of varying ages and even six-year-olds are reported to have taken up the sport. This is encouraging for the future of the game. Parents of these children should be particularly interested in the injury prevention and cure section so that they can help to guide their children in this important aspect. Young children often fail to recognize the importance of injury prevention.

I hope you enjoy the book and learn from its content, receiving as much pleasure out of the game of squash as I have received over the years.

David Pearson

Phil Kenyon of England. The wrist is kept firm with the racket head following through the ball to maintain good length. The shoulders are kept completely parallel to keep the chest square.

ONE

UNDERSTANDING THE SHOTS

THE · KNOCK-UP

Before beginning to play a game it is essential to knock-up with your opponent. This is a time not only for you to warm up but it also gives you a chance to assess your opponent.

Take advantage of the knock-up to gauge various factors which will help you once the game is under way. Carefully assess the speed of the ball off the walls, and that includes the side walls. Assess the temperature of the court and determine the height of the ceiling for playing lobs, looking out for any overhanging obstacles which may prevent such shots. And finally, use the knock-up to try and spot any weaknesses that your opponent may have, especially out of the back corners and playing the overhead on the volley.

If you spot an obvious weakness in your opponent's game it will effect the strategy of your game and the way you play your length shots. For example, if you were playing somebody considerably taller than you then you should make him bend and turn more by hitting the ball lower and with extra width.

THE · SHOTS

The Drive

The basic drive is an essential part of every squash player's game, no matter what level he plays at. The great players over the years have used the drive to full advantage and have been able to play the shot with length and width thus making it a winning stroke. Jonah Barrington used the shot effectively by getting height on the ball as a result of making full use of the front wall.

The most common fault club players make when playing the drive is to move to the ball in a direct line. You should avoid this at all costs because this approach to the ball will affect your balance, swing, and footwork. Instead, you should adopt the following important principles when moving to the ball to play the drive:

1. Keep your eye on the ball from the 'T'-position and don't move towards the ball until you are sure where it is going to bounce. Once you have decided on the ball's final position you should move into that area with your racket head up and in the 'ready' position.
2. Make sure your footwork is good. A right-handed player will move his left

UNDERSTANDING · THE · SHOTS

The basic forehand drive, played correctly with a low racket head.

foot forward into the shot on the forehand, and the right foot forward if playing a backhand drive. There may, however, be times when you get there with the wrong foot forward. Don't panic, just make sure your balance remains good and that your head and chest are facing the side wall, this will enable you to keep control of the shot and still manage to hit a good length. However, if you face the front wall with your head and chest the ball will probably come back directly at your body and this could prove costly.

The basic forehand drive played the wrong way. The racket head is too high.

Brett Martin's position is good for the high backhand volley. His shoulders are square to the side wall, he is well-balanced and the racket head is coming up underneath the ball to lift it high on the front wall so achieving length into the back corner.

SQUASH

The correct way to play the backhand drive. The knees are bent and the racket low.

The mistakes to be avoided when playing the drive are:

(a) Don't get too close to the ball because you will, invariably, end up playing the ball either in front of, or behind, your body. This will result in the loss of control of the shot.

(b) Don't hit the ball too hard and low over the tin. Make use of the height of the front wall to gain length. In fact, you shouldn't hit the ball too hard when under pressure. There's a great saying which you should remember: 'when it's tight, give it height'.

When playing the drive, either straight or cross court, aim to land the ball close to the rear of the service box and at a point where the red line meets the wall. As good practice, you can set up a matchbox (or something similar) near to that point, and aim to drive so that the ball hits the target.

Target practice is a great form of practice and is one used by the top coaches. It not only improves a player's ability, but it gives the coach an indication as to what progress the player is making. The more shots that hit the target the greater the racket control.

The purpose of the drive with length is to play the ball deep into the back corner and force a weak return. Many people *wrongly* believe the drive is a boring and

The wrong way to play the backhand drive. The racket is too high and the body too rigid.

SQUASH

negative shot. It is not, and if played correctly can be as exciting, and certainly as rewarding, as, for example, the nick.

Applying slice to the ball, by using an open racket face, will cause the ball to 'die' more quickly in the back corners after striking the side wall or floor. A ball hit with a flat face will sit up more. The right amount of cut must be allied to the correct height on the front wall.

Many of the top professionals, especially the likes of Rodney Martin, Tristan Nancarrow and Umar Hayat Khan apply a great deal of slice to their drives, and with great effect. You will notice that players from the hotter countries tend to play slice shots – it is more difficult to kill the ball in hotter climates with open-faced shots. They also impart a great deal of slice on the ball when playing it into the back corners.

Summing up Grip and swing are important when playing the drive, but there again, they are important in all squash shots. You should, by now, have mastered both. But the most important aspects of the drive are good footwork and balance. Get those right and you can always improvise. Make sure you are always well prepared for the shot and that you are in the right place at the right time.

The backhand drive played with perfect balance and follow through.

UNDERSTANDING · THE · SHOTS

A good backswing is important when playing the backhand drive.

SQUASH

A good follow through after playing the forehand drive.

Rodney Martin's racket head is prepared early with a firm wrist. He moves into the ball with eyes on the ball and the shoulder round to attack the ball aggressively.

SQUASH

Power in the forehand drive can be obtained by 'winding up' the shot.

Good balance is, once more, a key feature of the forehand drive.

The forehand drive.

The Lob

The lob is yet another essential shot crucial to every player's game, irrespective of his or her standard. Sadly, it is probably the least used of all squash strokes.

Understandably, the world's top players can execute the lob to perfection. But one of the finest exponents of the lob was Gogi 'The Spider' Alauddin. The diminutive Pakistani didn't hit the ball hard, but he had the knack of pushing the ball up the front wall to lob it with great height and precision into the back corners, thus opening up the court for him to attack from the front.

The aim of the lob is to hit it high on the front wall so that it rebounds high on the side wall behind the service box. If played successfully you will give yourself time to get back to the 'T'-position before your opponent can get to the ball.

The lob is normally played when under pressure which could be when you are off-balance, the ball is below the height of the tin, or under pressure on the service.

To avoid the elementary mistake of not getting the ball high enough on the front wall, thus inviting a volley, take note of the

The forehand lob. Note how close to the ground the racket head is.

The backhand lob.

The lob, played at full stretch.

following fundamentals for good lobbing:

1. Adopt a good stance position at the ball. Your knees and back should be bent and your bodyweight on your leading leg.
2. The racket head must start low, around knee-height, and your wrist should be firm. When carrying out the swing, the racket head must be brought under the ball as low as possible, and as near to the floor as possible.
3. Follow through immediately after striking the ball to gain maximum height as close to the out-of-court line as you can.
4. Don't hit the ball hard. It should be hit softly. In fact, the slower the better (but not too slow of course!) because it will give you time to recover to the 'T'-position and be ready for your opponent's return.
5. Try and play the lob with width to make the return difficult for your opponent thus turning a potential defensive position into an attacking one.

Don't forget that the lob can be played straight or cross court. The straight lob is one of the best shots in the game if played well. Apart from giving you the chance to get back to the 'T'-position, it denies your opponent the option of an easy attacking shot because there is no angle on the ball to hit it cross court. Playing a lot of straight lobs will test your opponent to the fullest – particularly his patience.

The lob can also be used as a strong tactical shot, particularly against players who strike the ball hard and fast because it slows the game down. You can therefore dictate the pace of the game which many 'hackers' don't like. A fast and hard hitter will have to make all the plays if you constantly play lobs to him, which will tire him.

Summing up Use the lob to give yourself time to recover if you are under pressure or off balance. Hit the ball high and slow on to the front wall. And use the lob to turn your potential defensive position into an attacking one.

Here, Martine le Moignian is well positioned to play the low volley with the wrist controlling the racket head and her right hand controlling her balance.

If the ball is played too late, ie from behind the player, it becomes very difficult to control and often ends up too high on the front wall.

The Boast

For many years the Boast was regarded as a defensive shot and was the shot you used 'as a last resort' when all else had failed. But in recent years the shot has been developed into a very effective one, even from the back of the court.

As with the drive, you will find the top players from the hotter countries will use the boast more as a means of 'killing' the ball. There are many different forms of boast, but the four most commonly used are: (a) the two-wall boast; (b) the three-wall boast, (c) the skid boast, (d) the trickle boast.

The two-wall boast This boast is played from just behind the service box, and can be played from in front of your opponent. It is played on to the side wall to land just above the tin on the front wall, with little pace and faded into the opposite side wall causing the ball to 'die' thus making sure your opponent has to move off the 'T' to retrieve it.

It is the leading stroke for making your opponent move, and it is certainly very tiring if you are on the receiving end of a lot of two-wall boasts.

Chris Robertson is a master of the two-wall boast and comes in quickly behind

Ideally, drop shots should only be attempted when you are well balanced and not stretched.

his opponent to cover anything hit from the front, or pick up any loose shot.

The three-wall boast This boast is played from just behind the service box and the intention is to play the ball on to the side wall, then the front wall, finally rebounding onto the opposite side wall and rolling out of the nick and onto the floor. It is an attacking shot, but you must ensure the ball hits the nick otherwise it will set your opponent up to play an attacking shot and therefore put you

under pressure.

Chris Dittmar is currently one of the finest three-wall boast players in the world.

The skid boast This shot is played from the back of the court and is hit high on the side wall and connects with the front wall, also at a high point, before rebounding on to the opposite side of the court from where you originally played the shot. It is designed to give you time to return to the 'T'; and get yourself out of trouble – if you're in it of course!

The skid boast is a shot more likely to be played by top class players rather than the average club player.

The trickle boast This is used at the front two corners and has to be hit delicately on to the side wall so that the ball 'dies' on the front wall and drops to the floor.

Like the drop shot, it is deceptive, so use it sparingly during a game to create that deception and catch your opponent unawares. To see the trickle boast played at its best, watch Ross Norman in action.

While the boast can be made from anywhere on the court, you are advised only to play it when in front of your opponent. However, you can boast from behind him if you want to force him to the front wall so that he has to make a return. But if you are employing this tactic, make sure the ball is tight to the side wall, otherwise your opponent will have a free attacking shot.

Another occasion when you might play the boast from behind your opponent is as a deception shot, holding the shot as long as possible until he has moved off the 'T'-position, and then sending him the wrong way with the boast from behind him.

Summing up The boast isn't a shot to use just for the sake of it. Only use it if you 'mean it'. It is a positive attacking shot which will move your opponent off the 'T'. Don't use it as a defensive shot unless it really is your only option. And finally, that golden rule, always make sure you are well balanced to make sure you have control of the racket head.

Jansher Khan is very low to the floor so that he is well balanced to play the drop. The footwork is perfect, enabling him to play the shot in balance.

The Volley

This can be one of the most exciting shots in the game of squash. Because you are playing the ball before it bounces you are giving yourself that feeling of playing an attacking shot and dominating the area around the 'T' by not letting the ball go through to the back of the court. But on saying all that, spectacular shots are not always that easy to play.

Because you are moving quickly to the ball in the first place, it makes the playing of the stroke that much harder. But if you can concentrate on getting in the correct position then a fast volleying game is certainly a spectacular one. This is particularly so if you can play the side-wall volley boast and/or the volley drop into the front corner with your opponent hopelessly out of position at the back of the court.

The difference between top class players and club players often comes down to the player's ability to take the ball early – to play the volley. But good, consistent volleying takes more than getting into the right place at the right time, it demands a very high level of fitness.

The technique for playing the volley is similar to the drive, and while many players are prepared to foresake a bit of accuracy on the volley, they are still keen to play the shot because of its attacking qualities and the chance that, being hurried, your opponent will rush his return and be forced into an error.

Many club players make the common mistake when playing the volley of going for the 'winner' with the volley. But this is not necessary. The volley itself is an attacking shot, as we have seen, and it often brings mistakes from your opponent which, in turn, produces the 'winner'. Overhitting is another fault frequently made when playing the volley. A full swing is not necessary – indeed, you

The volley – 'ready position'.

SQUASH

Note the follow through after the forehand volley.

When playing the backhand volley, keep your eye on the ball right up until the time it makes contact with the racket.

Timing is crucial with the backhand volley and weight should be on your front foot at the moment of impact.

The backhand volley. Stance is important and you must be standing side-on to the front wall.

wouldn't have time to play a full swing because of the speed you are moving into the ball. If you tried a full swing then you would probably lose your balance and that will not do the shot any good at all. It is better to use a shorter swing with a 'punching' action and your elbow bent. You then 'throw' the racket at the ball from the shoulder, thus giving you more control of the shot.

The drop volley is a spectacular shot but requires precision and exceptional balance. If your balance is not right, don't contemplate the shot and play an alternative, but with safety in mind.

The volley is one of the most important shots in your repertoire. Use it whenever you can. Don't let the ball bounce into the back of the court when a simple volley

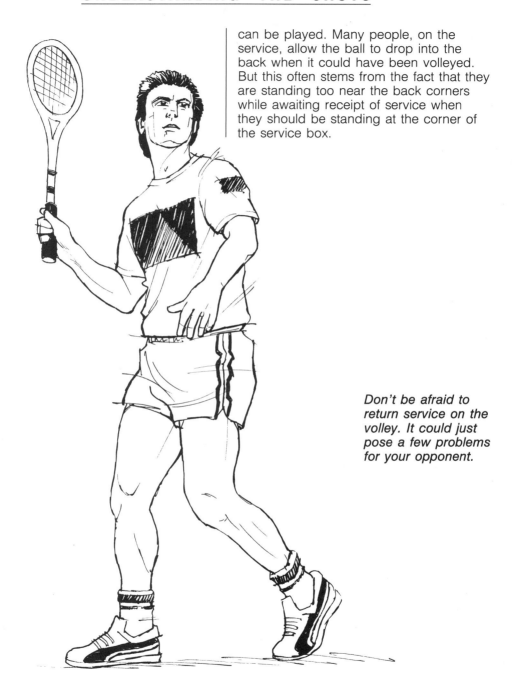

can be played. Many people, on the service, allow the ball to drop into the back when it could have been volleyed. But this often stems from the fact that they are standing too near the back corners while awaiting receipt of service when they should be standing at the corner of the service box.

Don't be afraid to return service on the volley. It could just pose a few problems for your opponent.

SQUASH

The forehand drop.

The Drop Shot

The secret of successful drop shots is to make sure the ball hits the front wall about 2in (5cm) above the tin and then drops close to the side wall. If you hit it any lower you will be prone to making an error. And if you don't let the ball bounce

The forehand drop played by a left-hander.

into a side wall then you are clearly giving your opponent a big advantage.

The drop should be played from around the 'T'-position whenever possible and with your opponent behind you. This forces him to run from a position deep in the court to make a recovery. Applying slice to the ball, as Rodney Martin often does, will cause the ball to find the nick and then 'die'. Other players take the

SQUASH

pace off the ball when playing the drop. They may not go for the winner by doing this, but gain a big advantage because their opponent has to do a lot of running to make the recovery each time.

When playing the drop you should remember the following important points:

1. Concentrate on early racket position. The head must be upright with your wrist 'cocked'. Never allow the racket head to hang around near to the ground. This will cause you to poke at the ball when playing the drop.
2. Get your balance right. Bend your knees and keep your eyes on the ball. If you are off-balance don't play the drop.
3. Make sure your racket face is open and travelling slightly behind the wrist so that you can feel the ball on the strings.

4. Aim to hit the front wall about 2in (5cm) above the tin and with the right amount of pace on the ball so that it doesn't bounce too far into the back of the court.
5. Make sure the ball bounces close to the side wall.

Don't play the drop too early in a rally. Try and tire your opponent out first. Play some shots to the back corners and get him used to going there. And when he seems to be tiring then bring the surprise element into play, and play the drop.

The backhand drop.

UNDERSTANDING · THE · SHOTS

Moving in to play the backhand drop. Keep your eyes on the ball.

Timing is important with the backhand drop – as it is with all shots.

The drop doesn't always have to be played from around the 'T'-position. It can be played from the back of the court and is particularly advantageous if you are trying to wrongfoot your opponent or he is obviously very tired. But a drop from so far back requires even greater precision. You can also play a cross-court drop if your opponent is well out of position and away from the 'T'. Always play a cross-court drop with plenty of cut so that the ball 'dies' low and does not bounce high off the floor or roll out of the nick.

The most important point to remember when playing the drop is be confident. And after playing the drop always return to the 'T'-position.

If you can master the drop, you will get more pleasure from it than you will any other shot in the game.

TWO

THE SERVICE

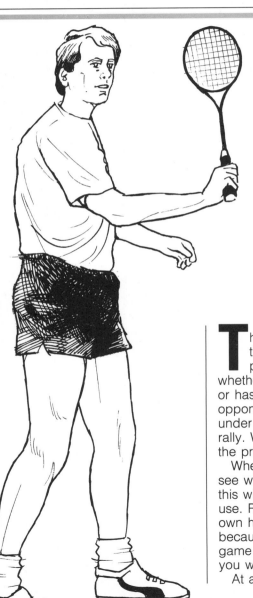

When preparing to receive service, do not look at your opponent, look for the ball at the earliest possible moment.

The service is vitally important. It is the stroke that starts the rally in progress. The serve also dictates whether your opponent can attack the ball or has to play defensively. If your opponent can attack the ball you will be under pressure from the first shot of the rally. Whereas if your serve is good then the pressure is on your opponent.

When serving, always have a look to see where your opponent is standing as this will determine what type of serve to use. Remember that the serve is in your own hands so make a good job of it because it is the only moment in the game that you can dictate how much time you want to take over the shot.

At a beginner's level the serve, if played

THE · SERVICE

Do not open your chest to the front wall when receiving a serve – a sure way to lose control.

well, can be a winning shot. But, unfortunately, no rallies take place and so the game's enjoyment is reduced. Whatever your playing level, the serve is important.

The main aim is to develop a serve that you can produce with some form of consistency. Once you can cope with that, a few variations can be used to surprise your opponent. The squash player will find the serve from the forehand side is easier to produce than the serve from the backhand side. The reason for this is that

on the forehand you are hitting across your body which gives you an angle to aim at. But on the backhand side you are actually serving with a forehand swing making the angle hard to obtain.

SQUASH

Notice the stretch Del Harris is making to the ball when under pressure. The open racket face is complemented by the wrist which controls the ball. His balance is perfect so giving him time to recover to the 'T'.

MAKING·THE·SERVICE

The basic principle of the serve is to get the ball tight to the side wall thus stopping your opponent volleying and forcing him into the back corners to return, you hope, a weak stroke. Try not to hit the side wall too early as the ball will only come out into the middle of the court presenting your opponent with an easy shot for an attempted winner. You must also not over-hit the serve as this will only bring the ball off the back wall and out into the middle. Again, this will give your opponent an easy shot. You will find most players tend to serve to their opponent's backhand when they first gain the serve. You may find the backhand is their stronger shot so think about your opponent's weaknesses.

The main point to remember is: the serve is not just a means of putting the ball into play. It is designed to allow you to put pressure on your opponent. Before we look at the different types of serve there are some basic principles to adhere to:

(a) Take your time in the service box.
(b) Look to see where your opponent is standing.
(c) Make sure you move on to the 'T' as soon as the ball has been struck.
(d) Vary the pace of the serve, *i.e.* some slow serves and some harder hit serves.
(e) When in the 'T'-position, follow the ball around to the back of the court and watch to be ready for your opponent's return.

An obvious point, of course, but don't forget that the lines in squash constitute a ball out of court; they are your 'enemies' when serving. An infallible way of losing a rally is to serve on or above the out-of-court line. Unlike tennis, it is not so easy

to win the rally outright with a service. Tactically, the emphasis is more on gaining the initiative.

RETURN·OF·SERVICE

When receiving service, the best place to stand is about 2ft (60cm) behind the corner of the service box keeping your body towards the corner of the front wall. You must watch your opponent serve the ball. Do not stare at the front wall because you can't react quick enough to the shot.

Prepare your racket early and move into position in relation to where the ball is going to be. Make sure you rotate your body so that your chest is square to the side wall. Having got yourself into the correct position, wait for the ball to reach its best point before striking it. Your racket must come under the ball which must be aimed high onto the front wall to achieve good length so you can move onto the 'T'. Always try to volley the ball to put pressure on your opponent right from the start.

Bad Habits

Listed below are the basic faults most people tend to have when receiving serve and how to correct them.

(a) Do not stand against the back wall, thus leaving you no room to swing your racket. If you do manage to return the ball, the return will be very weak giving your opponent an easy shot.

(b) Always try to volley the ball. Don't let it drop into the back corners as you will then not return the ball effectively, if at all.

(c) Do not go for winning shots too often as you will only make unforced errors. The best return is the straight volley down the wall to the back of the court.

(d) Don't open your chest to the front wall, try to keep your chest square to control the ball.

(e) Don't get too close to the side wall, you must have enough room to swing your racket. This will cause mis-timing or you could even miss the ball completely.

(f) Do not stand and watch where the ball is going to land. You must be watching and moving to the 'T' at the same time.

(g) Try to keep your body still at impact as this is the best way of controlling the ball. Moving as you strike the ball will only make the ball go to an area of the court you don't want it to.

The main reason the return of serve is so difficult is that it is basically a high volley which is one of the hardest shots in the game, even a good professional will find a high serve close to the side wall difficult to control.

Remember, be confident when striking the ball. Don't just close your eyes and hope for the best.

SQUASH

THE · DIFFERENT · TYPES · OF · SERVE

The basic serve

This is the serve that is used most often. It is a very simple serve that is easy to control and will not lose you many points but, at the same time, will put the minimum amount of pressure on your opponent.

Take position at the front of the service box, away from the side wall. Aim to hit the ball about 3ft (1m) above the cut line at medium pace making sure you put enough width into the shot so that the ball goes into the opposite side wall. This will put some pressure on your opponent. The width of this serve is of paramount importance because if the width is bad your opponent will attack the ball and put pressure on you.

The lob serve

This type of serve is the most commonly used one in the game. You must stand at the front of the service box, turn and check where your opponent is. Make sure you have an open racket face and serve the ball high on to the front wall to rebound across the court, making sure the ball lands just under the out of court line on the opposite side wall.

The secret of a good lob serve is to try to put as little pace on the ball as possible so that the ball is dropping at a steep angle when it reaches your opponent.

Del Harris is showing good footwork with the racket prepared early to hit the ball with an open racket face. Notice how good his balance is and his eyes are, once again, watching the ball.

The hard hit serve

This serve is used as a surprise, causing your opponent to react slowly or, if he is out of position, struggle to return the ball.

Again, stand at the front of the service box checking that you are going to strike the ball with a flat face. Strike the ball hard just above the cut line making sure the ball is fading into the side wall causing your opponent to react quickly. Move directly to the 'T' to punish a weak return. Ensure that the racket face is not open as the ball will fly out of court giving away the point.

The surprise serve (or tactical serve)

This type of serve is used as a surprise tactic either for an outright winner or to force a weak return for you to capitalize on. Use this serve only once or twice in a match.

1. Serve the ball straight at the body of your opponent who will be expecting a normal serve. If he does not react quick enough, the ball will strike his body or he will play the ball in the tin. Or:
2. Serve the ball down your opponent's wrong side. Serve the ball behind his back causing him to have to take the ball on the wrong side. If you serve on his forehand, for example, he will have to play the shot with his backhand, possibly causing panic in the shot.

Finally, if you are tired, always use the lob serve as this gives you time to rest and take in more oxygen. If your opponent is tired, get into position quickly to force him to receive as quickly as possible so that he can't recover, thus giving you the initiative and confidence.

THREE

DOMINATING THE 'T'

While this area of the game is important, it can be dangerous if you don't know what you are doing. There are various ways of dominating the 'T' but there are a few basic principles which you must adopt:

(1) Playing tight squash. If you put the ball tight to the walls and into the front and back corners you basically will never leave the 'T'. You let your opponent do all the running and you will therefore be in the dominant position.

(2) Moving back to the 'T'-position. This is important because most average club players tend to hit the ball and look to see where it has bounced before moving to the 'T'. You must move as the ball is travelling so that you are on the 'T' when your opponent is striking the ball.

(3) The most important shot for 'T'-domination is the volley. If you are volleying, you are keeping position as you never usually have to leave the short-line across the middle of the court.

(4) Balance is the real key to gaining 'T'-domination. If you are balanced with a good base between your feet, then with one stride you can return to the 'T'-position.

(5) Never leave the 'T'-area more than you have to. Remember, big long strides are the secret, not short little strides, as these make you leave the 'T' area too far behind and don't give you enough time to recover.

(6) If you do not volley you will never be in position. Remember, the more pressure put on in this area, the more running your opponent has to do.

(7) If your opponent is on the 'T', remember that if you have hit the ball through the middle, you are not entitled to be anywhere near your opponent. You must give room for your opponent to swing the racket with no interference. If you do rush in, you will only get hit with the racket, causing injury.

(8) If you feel that your opponent is too close to you when on the 'T', stop, don't play the shot. However, if this is the case, the point is the striker's, it is not a let.

(9) When the ball is in the middle of the court the striker is entitled to force his

DOMINATING · THE · 'T'

A forehand drive from the 'T'.

opponent into the back of the court and then play his shot. The person who is being forced back must move back towards the back wall. If he does not, a point is once more awarded to the striker.

Remember that the 'T'-area is the most important part of the court, so don't give it up lightly. Compete for position (but not physically). If you are never on the 'T', tiredness will set in quickly causing you to lose the game.

A final word on the domination of the 'T'. Never stand still after you have hit the ball – move back to the 'T' whenever possible to cover the shot.

SQUASH

Dominating the 'T' – a vital part of the game of squash.

DOMINATING · THE · 'T'

Vying for the most advantageous position around the 'T' sometimes can lead to problems and a ruling from the referee. The winning tactic is always to return to the 'T' as fast as possible after every shot to 'stake your claim'.

FOUR

TACTICAL PLAY

Once you have reached a standard of play where you are able to control the ball and place it where you want in the court, the next step is to learn about the tactical side of the game.

The main tactic is always to hit the ball away from your opponent, causing him to move to the furthest part of the court to retrieve the ball. So, here we will look at where to put the ball from various shots hit at you, and where to try to put the ball when under pressure.

PLACING · THE · BALL

The first tactic we will look at is where to place the ball on your drives.

Straight drives from the front of the court

The first drives we will look at are the ones from the front corners on both the backhand and forehand.

When striking the ball, your objective is to move your opponent off the 'T', pushing him into one of the back corners. To achieve this you must strike the ball on the cut line or higher, and as close to the

side wall as possible. This will automatically cause your opponent to move off the 'T' and thus give you pole position. The ball must land within at least four floorboard widths from the side wall thus preventing your opponent from volleying. After the ball has reached the back of the court you must get to the 'T'. Don't just stand and watch the ball after making your shot – get to the 'T'.

Straight drives from he back of the court

This is the one area of the court from where many people find it difficult to return the ball. Normally, when you are in the back of the court your opponent is on the 'T' so your return has to be exceptionally good in order to apply pressure.

Unfortunately, a lot of players try to hit the ball too low on the front wall which only brings the ball back to the short line, so your opponent then has a vast choice of shots to play with you out of position. Therefore, you must try to hit the ball as high as you can onto the front wall and follow through on your stroke to make sure the ball hits the back of the court.

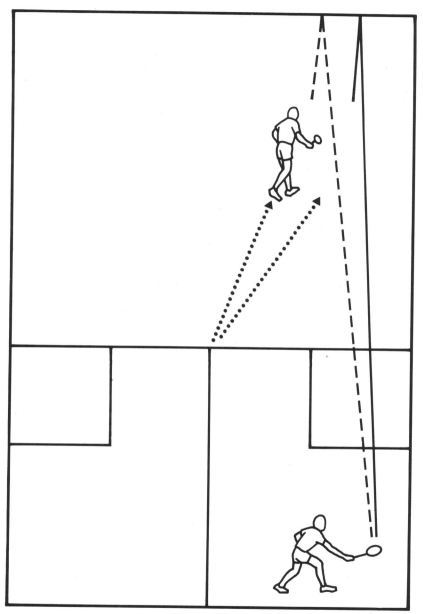

Once more, try to keep the ball as close as possible to the side wall. If you achieve this, you will have gained the initiative and will then be able to put pressure on your opponent.

Straight drives from the front of the court.

SQUASH

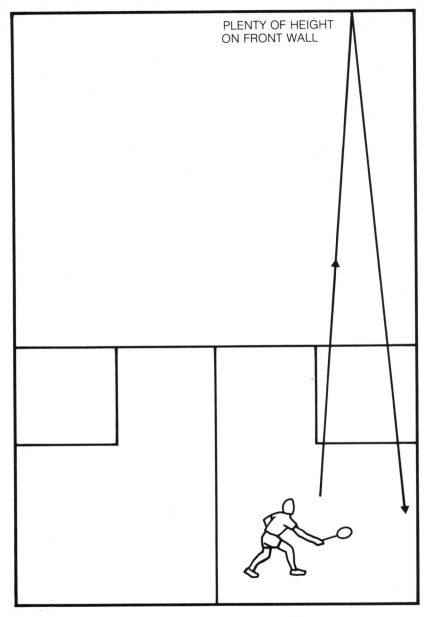

Cross-court drives: front and back
Shot A: cutline cross-court
Shot B: plenty of height on the front wall.

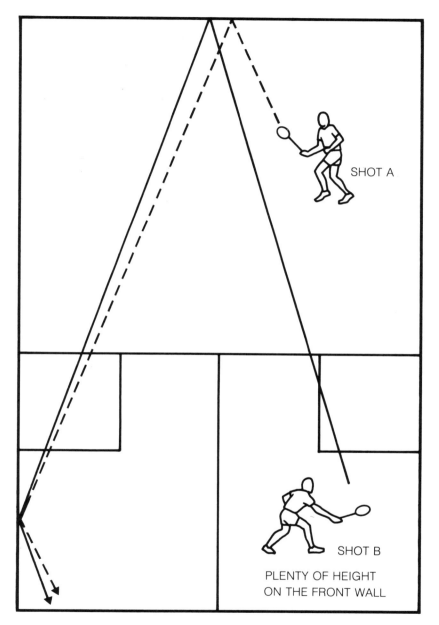

SHOT A

SHOT B

PLENTY OF HEIGHT
ON THE FRONT WALL

Cross-court drives: front and back

The cross-court drive can be one of the best shots in the game if hit into the correct area of the court. However, if not it can be one of the worst shots in the game. Like so many other shots, hitting the cross-court drive is often an attempt to get your opponent off the 'T'-position. When playing this type of shot you should stick to the following conditions:

(a) If your opponent is on the 'T', then the cross-court drive must hit the back of the service box before 'dying' in one of the back corners. To achieve this, the ball must be hit on the cut line or above. The height gained on the front wall dictates how far back into the court it will land.

(b) When you have a lot of time to play your shot you can play an attacking cross-court which is hit low above the tin but still aims to land behind the service box. This type of cross-court drive is used when trying to win the rally.

(c) When you are under pressure in the corners you must not rush your shot or try to hit the ball at a fast pace or swing the racket too quickly. Remember, when under pressure, slow down and lift the ball high on to the wall to give yourself time to re-adjust.

(d) Don't use the cross-court drive all the time. Use it sparingly. Often a straight ball is the better shot.

The drop shot

The drop is a shot that causes a lot of problems for players because they often don't have the confidence to play the stroke. But, you need the drop in your repertoire of shots if you are going to be a successful player.

If the drop is played from the correct areas in relation to your opponent's position, it doesn't have to be inch perfect. However, your main problem is in trying to hit the ball too low above the tin, or playing the shot from the wrong areas of the court. The following dos and don'ts of the straight and cross-court drop shots will help:

(a) The best drop to play is the straight drop when your opponent is stuck in either of the back two corners of the court and is forced to play a boast. In this instance, he is well out of position so you move up to the front of the court and play the drop about 2in (5cm) above the tin and let the ball drop into the side wall. Don't threaten to play a drop and then hit the ball to the back of the court, thus playing back to your opponent.

(b) Another easy occasion to play the drop is when your opponent has struck the ball into the middle of the court and he is behind you. Once again, just push the ball to either of the front two corners. Make sure the ball is tight to the side wall as this will cause your opponent to move around you and therefore is put under pressure. Once again, your point of aim on the front wall should be approximately 2in (5cm) above the tin.

(c) Do not play drops from the back of the court unless your opponent is out of position. It is too risky and brings too many unforced errors, thus giving your opponent easy points.

(d) Try not to play the drop when under pressure and your balance is poor

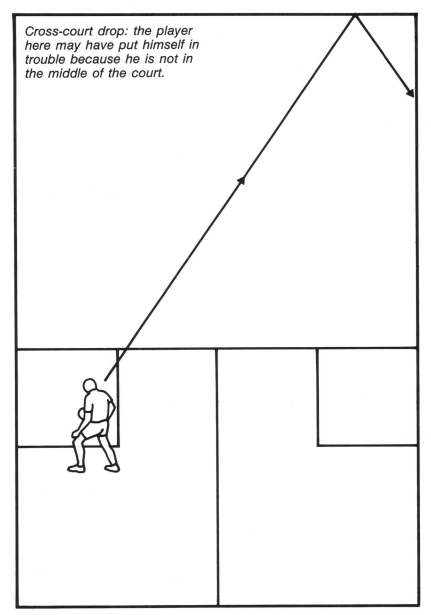

Cross-court drop: the player here may have put himself in trouble because he is not in the middle of the court.

because you will inevitably play too low. You will see professionals play drops when under pressure, but don't forget they have the ball control to play such a delicate shot.

The cross-court drop should be played when you are in the middle of the court and your opponent is behind you. Make sure the ball is played close to the nick or is tight to a side wall. Remember, though, that if you play the shot poorly, it opens up the court for your opponent to step in and gain the advantage.

A final word on the drop; never be frightened to play the shot and make sure you are positive with the stroke. You are, after all, trying to play a winner. If you are not confident and positive you will play a bad shot and the initiative will pass to your opponent.

Volleys

Even at the highest level of squash, this is the one shot that determines the superiority of one player over another. Professionals 'take the ball early' in order to apply pressure.

The shot takes a lot of control in order to produce a good position of the ball on the court and the important rule is: if you volley, don't leave the 'T'. Always make sure you are in control of the rally. Also, never try to hit the ball too hard as good placement is the secret of successful volleying. The main principles of volleying are:

(a) Never let the ball go past you if you are in a position to reach it.

(b) If hitting length on the volley, make sure the ball strikes the front wall above the cut line in order to let the ball travel to one of the back corners. If the ball is hit too low, it will only bounce half court and thus either put pressure on yourself, or possibly give away a penalty point as a result of your crossing the line of the ball. This would then prevent your opponent from getting clear access and stop him from striking the ball onto the front wall.

(c) The time to hit a low hard volley is when your opponent is at the front and you are on the 'T' thus giving him no chance to reach the ball. When in this position, don't rush your shot as this may cause you to hit the ball against the tin. Instead, wait for the ball to reach you and calmly strike it away for a winning low volley.

(d) Like the drop shot, if you have your opponent 'buried' deep in one of the corners, and the return is weak, you should play a volley drop, forcing him to move forward quickly. Do not hit the ball back. If you have a lot of time, look up to see where your opponent is. Sometimes players stand and don't cover their shot(s). In this case, all you have to do is keep the ball above the tin to win the point.

(e) One of the biggest problems is the return of serve on the volley. Never let the ball bounce into the back corner as it won't bounce out, causing you to lose the point without a rally taking place. You must always try to volley the serve straight down the side wall thus applying pressure on your opponent at the very start of the rally.

The Boast

Tactically, the boast is one of the most important shots in the game. It is the shot used to move your opponent around the court to the point that he eventually becomes tired and makes weak returns, thus establishing you in control of the rally and/or game.

When boasting, remember that it is an attacking shot and not a shot to be used solely for the purpose of keeping the ball in play. Never use a boast that is high on the front wall. This will only set up your opponent for an attacking shot and a likely winner.

The back-wall boast should only be used in the direst circumstances. It will, if hit high and rising, usually ensure the continuation of the rally, but the initiative has certainly passed to your opponent, unless fortune is smiling on you.

TACTICAL · PLAY

Now that the basic shots have been discussed it is a matter of being able to bring all the different aspects together into a match situation. But that is something that cannot be put on to the pages of a book. Match experience is invaluable and it is only then that you will see the advantages and disadvantages of playing the various shots at the right and wrong times.

After a game, always sit down for five minutes or so and analyse the match, no matter whether you have won or lost. But the best experience can be gained by watching top class players in action. Using your own basic knowledge of the different shots, watch how and when they play them. One thing that will become obvious is that squash is not only about shot making, it is very tactical, as each player looks for the all-important opening.

The mind game

This is an area of your game which is so important, both tactically and for your concentration. You must always be thinking of what you are doing. If your mind is wandering then your game will suffer.

During a game, concentrate on one point at a time. Don't think about how far behind, or ahead, you are. And if you are trailing, don't let your head drop. Your lack of confidence will be a considerable boost to that of your opponent.

One piece of good advice; when receiving serve, always play with safety in mind – don't play an outrageous shot, because if you do and you lose, then you lose a point. You should go for those match-winning shots when you are serving because then, if they come off, you win a point and if they don't, well, all you lose is the serve.

Finally, don't let any outside distractions interfere with your game, think only of what you are doing on court.

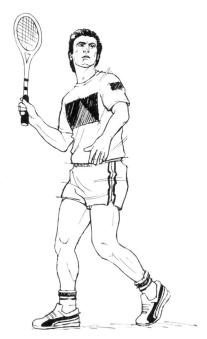

Overleaf – The ball is very low to the floor causing Bryan Beeson to move in low getting down to the ball and keeping the wrist firm. He also has a good position to return to the 'T' from.

GOING · INTO · A · MATCH

The following are important pointers you should consider both before you actually start your match and once you have got play under way. They are very important to your approach and attitude. Most people like to win matches, and these pointers are for winners:

The warm-up

The warm-up is crucial to all sports, and particularly squash. You should have done your preparatory stretching exercises before going on to court to loosen up those muscles. You should also make sure you have got your mind in the right frame. If you haven't warmed up properly, you

can easily find yourself losing the first game without realizing what has happened. And recovery then becomes increasingly hard because the initiative has already passed to your opponent.

You should be like a sprinter when you go on to the squash court and be ready to go as soon as 'the starting gun is fired' or, in the case of squash, as soon as the ball is first in play.

I know many people are limited in the time they have to play squash and may be getting in a game on their way home from work, but it only takes a couple of minutes to stretch those muscles before going on court. You must always warm them up. In addition to helping your suppleness on court, the warm-up will help reduce the risk of injury.

The knock-up

The knock-up is used to warm the ball up, but you should also use it to have a look at your opponent. The following points in your opponent's play should be checked out during the knock-up:

(a) Does he hold his racket correctly? If not, he will be weak in the back corners or to any balls played close to the walls.

(b) Is your opponent overweight? If he is, then he will have problems with drop shots and boasts.

(c) Is your opponent wearing bandages? If so, it means he probably has an injury or alternately, is trying to get some sympathy from you. Don't have any of it . . . if he's that badly injured he shouldn't be playing in the first place!

During the knock up you should always hit balls of varying lengths, particularly those to the back of the court so that you can obtain your length and also test the speed of the ball and court at the same time.

Overcoming nerves

Many people suffer from nerves when they first go on to court. The following useful tips should help you overcome this problem if it affects you at the start of a game:

(a) At the start, make sure you hit the ball consistently to the back of the court thus ensuring you have a good rhythm to your swing. Don't go for silly shots early on. You will probably lose early points and this will cause even more panic.

(b) Don't put pressure on yourself by expecting to win. Go into a match in the knowledge that you will do your best. The winning will come naturally after that.

(c) Remember that you are playing the ball that is hit to you and not playing your opponent. Don't be intimidated by your opponent. He may be better than you, but if you let him know you are afraid of him then he will be even better. So, put out of your mind who you are playing and just make sure you play the ball. If possible, always try to keep the ball close to the wall. That way your opponent is well away from you.

Coping with oxygen debt

Oxygen debt is caused when there is not enough oxygen reaching the blood stream thus making your breathing short. Consequently you cannot control your breathing.

The natural instinct when you are in this situation is to go for a winning shot but, being in the condition you are, you will invariably play a weak shot. If you find yourself in this position, lift the ball high on to the front wall to give yourself some time to recover, get to the 'T', and take in a few more gulps of air.

Coping with pressure

If you are at full stretch on the retrieving end of a rally, you should try to relieve the pressure by hitting the ball straight down the walls to the back of the court. Don't hit cross court, which is what most people do when under pressure. This opens up the court and gives your opponent too many options to hit the ball to any part of the court he or she chooses, and then you will be under even more pressure.

Relaxation

This is a very important word to remember when you go on court. If you are relaxed, your movement will be smooth, the swing of your racket will be uninhibited and most importantly, your mind will be on the game.

FIVE

FITNESS TRAINING

One of the mistakes people make when they take up squash as a sport is thinking that it will make them fit, helping them in their daily routine both mentally and physically. However, this is not so.

You must be fit before you actually decide to play squash, otherwise problems could occur. For example, when you are engaged in a rally, your heart can beat at up to 200 times a minute which causes an oxygen debt. So, as you can see, your body must be able to cope with such rigours.

Squash is an explosive type of movement. One minute you may take short strides to reach the ball quickly to catch your opponent out of position. And the next you can be taking long strides to use your speed in an economical manner. You also have to keep yourself well balanced and able to return to the 'T' when under pressure from your opponent who may have hit a tight shot. Consequently, you need strong legs to be able to cope with the continued strain on the thigh and calf muscles, not to mention the pressure put on your lungs and increased heart rate.

The fitter you are to begin with, the more you will be able to increase the oxygen intake into your body to control the oxygen debt. And the fitter you are, the quicker you can recover and get ready to play for the next point.

A good breakdown between muscle use and cardiovascular use during a game of squash is 30% to 70%. It is therefore more important to have good recovery powers with your breathing than with your muscles. Don't forget, the average club player is on court for approximately 40 minutes at one time while a top international player can be on court for up to two hours. The muscle recovery aspect, then, is not as crucial to the club player as it is to the international player.

We will now look at various forms of fitness training for the squash player, starting with pressure routines with a ball.

COURT · ROUTINES · WITH · THE · BALL

Drive and boast

This exercise it the most important at 'middle club' standard. It requires one

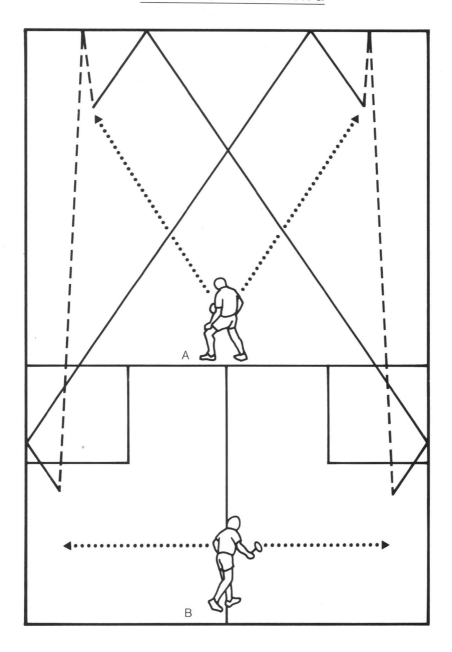

Drive and boast routine
A worker: hitting straight drives
B feeder: boasting to the front of the court.

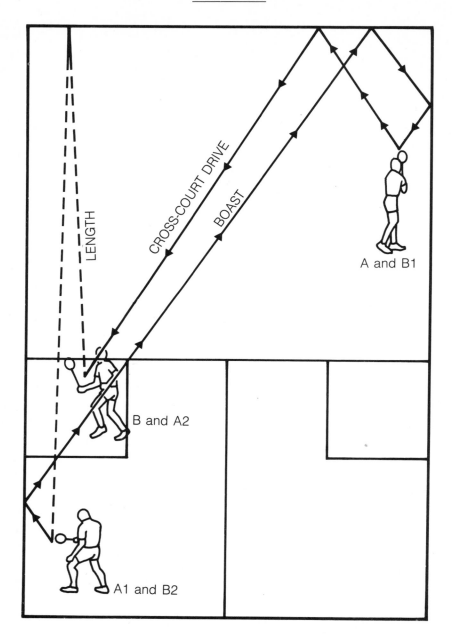

Cross-court drive, length and boast routine. This is a strenuous work out practising three shots at once. A plays to B, B plays to A1, A1 plays to B1, and so on.

player to stand at the back of the court (B) and the other on the 'T' (A). B must then play a boast from the forehand back corner to the front backhand corner making sure B moves from the 'T' to the front backhand and therefore plays a backhand drive down the wall so that the ball is close to the wall. It must bounce behind the service box. He must then return to the 'T'-position ready for the next stroke from B which this time will be a backhand boast to the front forehand. The ball is then returned down the wall in the same way as the backhand.

The main points for player A to remember are:

(a) Strike the ball around the cut line to obtain a good length.

(b) The ball must be kept close to the wall in order to put pressure on the opponent.

(c) Always return to the 'T'-position after playing the shot.

And the important points for player B to remember are:

(a) Try to keep the ball as low over the tin as possible.

(b) The ball must bounce no further out from either side wall than the fourth floorboard.

(c) Don't let the ball drop too far into the back corners of the court, otherwise the boast becomes too hard to play.

Practise each position for ten minutes, by which time your body will be warm enough and ready to move to the next, slightly harder, routine.

When practising, start with a fairly easy routine and gradually work up to the harder routines which will put extreme demands on you physically.

Cross-court drive, length and boast

Again with one person at the back of the court (B) and the other on the 'T' (A). Player B plays a boast while player A plays a cross-court drive to behind the service box back to B1. B1 then hits the ball back to length while A now moves to the back (A1) and plays a boast causing his opponent to move to the front (B2). He then hits the cross-court drive. Try to keep this routine going for five minutes, alternating positions at the front and back of the court. Try not to make any errors during the five minute routine.

This exercise will make your breathing difficult to cope with, but after a minute's rest it should return to normal.

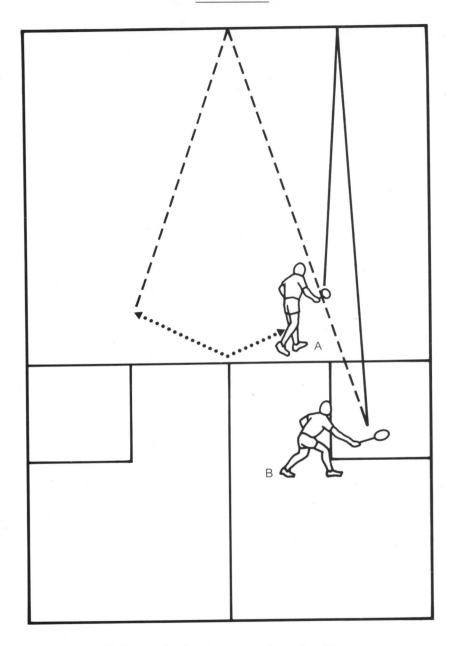

Volley to the back corners from the 'T' routine. A worker: hitting volleys deep into the back of the court. B feeder.

The drop shot routine
A feeder. B worker.

Volley to the back corners from the 'T'

Yet again, one player stands at the 'T'-position (A) while the other is at the back of the court behind the service box (B). B either feeds the ball down the wall or cross court. A then has to try and volley the ball straight, keeping it close to the wall. The most important feature of this exercise for player A is that he must not let the ball bounce past him off the front wall, he must volley it.

Practise the routine for five minutes and then swap roles.

The Drop Shot

One person stands by the side wall on the forehand (A) and feeds the ball gently onto the front wall. Meanwhile, his practice partner (B) takes up position on the 'T'.

He has to move forward (B1) to play a drop shot making the ball finish as close to the wall as possible. He must then return to the 'T' as quickly as possible.

The ball is fed again in the same way and should be repeated 20 times before reversing roles. The purpose of this exercise is to improve mobility around the 'T', as well as getting the feel of the delicate nature of the drop shot.

Also, alternate between feeding and playing on the forehand and backhand. When you have finished the exercise your thigh muscles will be sore. But they should recover after about two minutes.

The foregoing routines should take about 40 minutes in total to complete and should be practised once a week. You will soon show a marked improvement in your general fitness. They will also teach you the importance of moving quickly and economically around the squash court.

Gwain Briars is on his toes moving forward watching the ball with the racket head well-prepared and a firm wrist to control the stroke.

LIMITED · GAMES

These are exercises in which the game of squash is played, but with limitations. Both practice partners must play the ball to set areas of the court, as shown in the following examples.

Playing the ball to length routine. All shots are played from behind the mid-court line.

Playing the ball to length

Both players have to hit the ball, either straight or cross court, to the back of the court behind the short line but tight to either side wall and away from the middle.

The idea of this exercise is to make sure you try to volley the ball and thus keep your opponent deep in the back corners forcing loose returns and errors. The limited game should be played up to nine points using the normal scoring method.

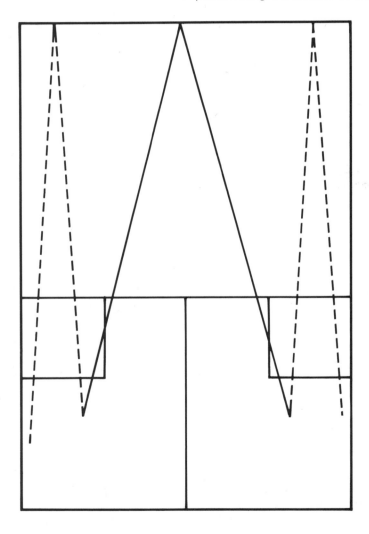

Short and long

The game is started with one person in the back of the court (A) and the other person in the front (B). Again, the one at the front does most of the work! Player A has to hit the ball in front of the short line while B has to return each ball to the back, either straight or across court, but as tight to the walls as possible. The game is played up to nine points and then the roles are reversed.

Short and long routine.

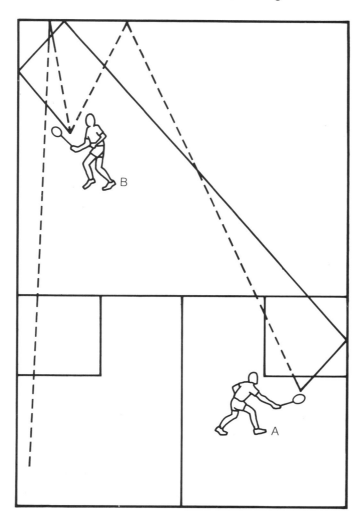

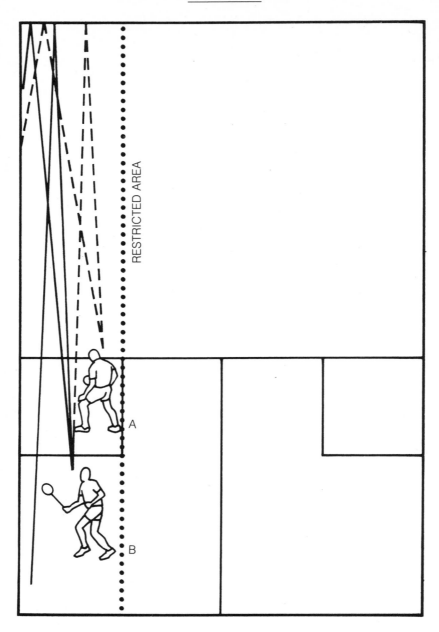

RESTRICTED AREA

A

B

Alley Games.

Alley game

This limited game is the most important 'restricted game' in squash. It is started with one player standing on the short line (A) and the other at the back of the service box on the forehand side (B). The person on the short line serves to the opponent, who has to return the ball down the wall, either short or long. The rally continues with each player trying to keep the ball as tight to the wall as possible. The rally is lost when the ball hits the tin or lands above the out of court line. The ball is also out when it bounces more than 6ft (2m) from the side wall.

When you have finished playing a game on the forehand side, transfer to the backhand side and again, keep the ball as close to the wall as possible to force your opponent into making errors.

These limited games and routines are important to your general fitness level, and are also designed to improve your ball control. This will enable you to place the ball into good areas within the court which will consequently mean you don't have to do too much running.

GHOSTING

These are other exercises for general fitness. Ghosting (or court sprints) is a series of exercises without the ball. This area of fitness is for keen squash players who thrive on being at peak fitness and can cope with the strain the exercises put on their bodies.

These exercises will improve your mobility around the court. They will enable you to last longer in rallies, so reducing the risk of you making silly mistakes because of tiredness.

All the routines should be done in sets and the fitter you get, the more sets you should attempt and with less of a breather in between. Ideally, initially, they should be attempted with a 45-second break between each exercise. However, when you first attempt court sprints, don't aim for any more than five sets. There will always be plenty of time to build the number up as you get fitter.

When sprinting, take long bounding strides as opposed to short steps. The latter will make you tired very quickly. The long bounding strides will improve your quality of movement and, at the same time, will conserve your energy. That word 'quality' is an important one. The better the exercise is carried out, the more benefit you will gain in your movement around the court.

Attention to detail is very important: always make sure your feet are in the correct position when ghosting; ensure your eyes are focussed on the area where the ball would be if playing a match; bend correctly when swinging; and finally, move in a crab-like manner or as Jonah Barrington would say, 'Hunt the ball'. Always recover to the 'T'-area as quickly as possible.

The following 30-minute ghosting programme has been designed for your increased general fitness. It is recommended that you carry it out twice a week.

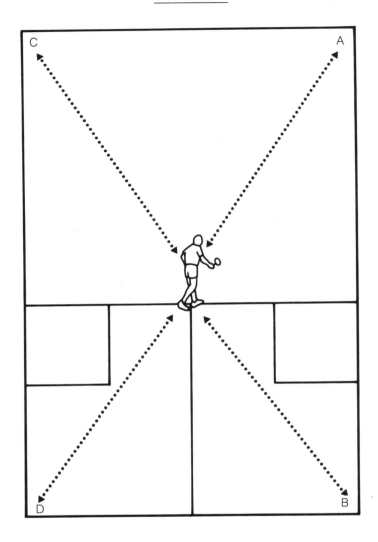

Court sprint no.1

Stand on the 'T' in a 'ready' position. Start your movement into the front forehand corner and play a 'shadow' forehand drive then recover to the 'T'-position by running backwards in a crab-like manner then move to the back of the court to play a forehand drive. Again move back to the 'T' and do the same on the backhand side. Carry out this routine for one minute. Take a 45-second break and then continue. The court sprint should be at approximately three-quarter pace and you should be concentrating on those long bounding strides we have already mentioned. Carry on until you have completed five sets, which should take approximately 10 minutes, including your 'breathers'.

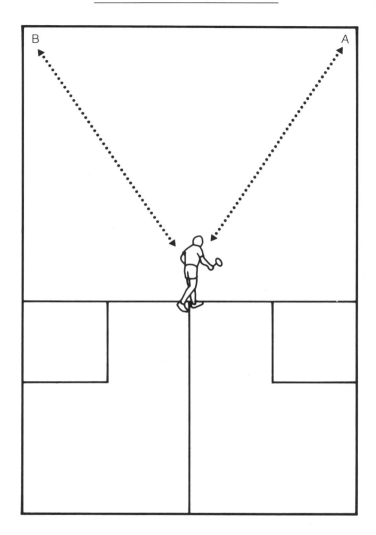

Court sprint no.2

Start at the 'T'-position and move into the front forehand corner, back to the 'T', and then into the front backhand corner.

Repeat this for one minute then take your 45-second breather. Carry out this exercise just twice.

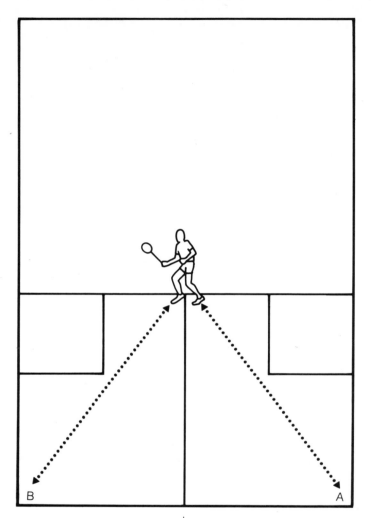

Court sprint no.3

Start at the 'T'-position and move into the forehand back corner, then back to the 'T', and then into the backhand back corner and so on for one minute. Again, just two sets are all that you need to do. But it is important that you maintain that crab-like movement as you move around the court.

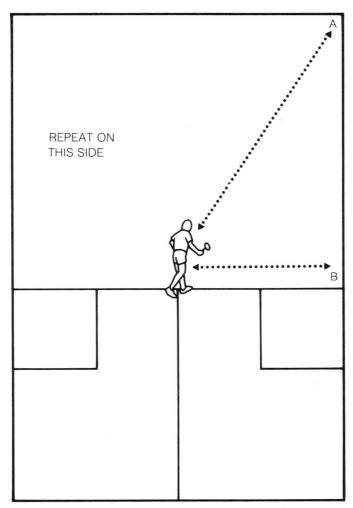

REPEAT ON
THIS SIDE

A

B

Court sprint no.4

Once more the starting position is the 'T'. Your first movement this time is to the front forehand corner, back to the 'T', and then across to the side wall on the forehand side, back to the 'T' and so on for one minute. Rest, and then repeat on the backhand side. Repeat both sides twice.

Those four sprints should take you approximately half an hour. At the end,

your legs will feel very tired as they will be full of lactic acid. It is therefore important that you warm down to relieve your legs of the acid and to prevent them from feeling stiff the next day.

After about a month of court sprints you will start to see a general improvement in your overall fitness and, of course, you will find them easier to carry out. It is at this point that you want to start increasing your number of sets and reducing the rest period in between each.

FITNESS · AWAY · FROM · THE · SQUASH · COURT

The court sprints which we have already discussed, don't have to be on a squash court. They can be practised on any area similar to a squash court. But there are many other exercises which can be carried out away from the squash court.

A lot of squash enthusiasts like to run to keep fit. They find that training on the court can be too claustrophobic and, instead, prefer to get out into the open air.

There are various forms of running you can do off court. There is track running, sprinting, and long distance running. All such activities should entail repetitive work or short runs of, say, three miles – not that you would sprint for three miles of course!

Excessively long distances are of no real benefit to the squash player because they do nothing to aid his movement around the court. Long distance running will help to make you fit but will make you very slow around the squash court.

When running, try to run on soft surfaces rather than hard roads. These can cause injury, keeping you off the

The perfect position for the return of serve. Jahangir Khan's racket head is high, his shoulders are square, wrist cocked and eyes never taken off the ball.

squash court for months. The lack of cushioning on hard roads can put excessive pressure on your calves, knees and back.

Detailed below are some suggested training routines away from the court. Remember; start off with only a few repetitive sets and increase the number as you get fitter.

Track work

You find that most professional squash players tend to do track work more than basic running for their fitness. The most popular distance is 400 metres (one full circuit). There will be a local athletics club not too far from your home and if you explain to them why you would like to use their facilities, they will probably be only too pleased to accommodate you.

Before we look at a typical 400 metres routine, it is worth pointing out that one of the game's all-time greats, Geoff Hunt of Australia, was capable of running thirty 400 metres, each in 70 seconds, and with only a one minute break between each. It is that sort of dedication which turns players into greats. You will not be expected to reach those levels of fitness, but it does highlight the importance of being super-fit at the top of the ladder.

A basic routine for you to work to would be as follows:

(a) Start with a set of 5 × 400 metres trying to achieve a time of 80 seconds for each and with a one minute break between each run. It is important that each lap is covered in 80 seconds (or thereabouts). It is no good doing the first in 80 seconds, the next in 90, then 85 and so on. You have to pace yourself so that you get your breathing consistent.

(b) As the weeks go by, increase the number of 400s until you have reached 10 sets in 80 seconds. After that, your next goal should be to bring the 10 sets down to 70-second laps. It should take you about 3 to 4 months of regular running to achieve this. Even before you reach that target you will notice an improvement in your general fitness and mobility around the court.

You should aim to get onto the track at least once a week, but ideally twice a week will be of more benefit to you.

We will now move on to short distance running, covering three miles at a time.

When covering this sort of distance it is important to try to run as fast as you physically can. Running as fast as your body will allow helps to keep your heart rate high. But don't forget, we said earlier that you don't have to sprint the full three miles.

A good way of running on this distance to work on your speed is to sprint for 100 metres, then slow down for 200 metres, and then go back to a 100 metre sprint, repeating this throughout the full distance. Remember, all forms of training are being geared to your ability as a squash player. That is why a change to and from sprinting during your run is important. It will again be invaluable to your mobility on the squash court.

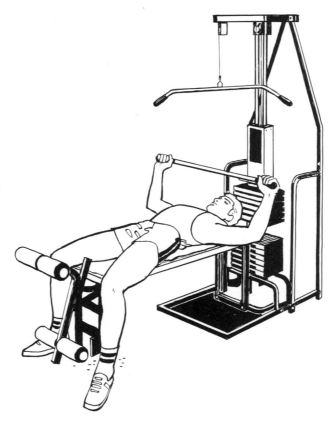

FITNESS · TRAINING

Weight training

Weight training can be very useful to the squash player, just as it can to any sportsman. But it must be carried out carefully and with a specially worked out programme for your sport's needs. There is no sense in developing muscles that you aren't going to need when playing squash.

The important thing to remember is don't use excessively heavy weights. More repetitions at lighter weights give greater benefit. Heavy weights will develop too much muscle and that will destroy your mobility around the court.

However, proper use of weights as part of your training will help to develop more strength in your legs and improve your cardio-vascular system. These will all help your mobility around the court and general fitness, which is what you should be striving for constantly as a squash player.

You are well advised to join a gym club and seek advice from the instructor who will work out a programme for your individual needs. He is there to give advice – take it. And whatever you do, work with weights under supervision. Weight training can be dangerous if not treated with respect and if strict safety guidelines are not adhered to. But if you do take up this form of training the benefits to you as a squash player will be there for you to see when you get on the court.

Using a multi-gym can be beneficial to the squash player, but obviously bulk is the last thing you need, so a high number of repetitions with low weights is the best approach.

Food and squash

When you eat before a game of squash is very important. Eat too close to your game and you will be uncomfortable. Indigestion is a likely outcome, followed by, no doubt, defeat – unless your opponent has eaten more than you! Some people don't eat anything before a game. But this can also have an adverse effect and can cause dizziness. So, what do you eat before a game of squash? And when do you eat it? The following very rough guidelines will help:

(a) Try to eat at least four hours before your game. This gives plenty of time for you to digest the food.

(b) Try to eat carbohydrates; potatoes, pasta etc. These will improve your stamina and help you to last longer when playing.

(c) Take an intake of liquid about half an hour before playing. Water is suitable, but some form of health drink is better.

After your match, make sure you have another intake of liquid to replace the minerals and water lost during the physical exercise of playing.

Finally, many of the exercises outlined are to be used purely as a guide. You may find some of them are not suited to you. Pick out the ones that are suited and/or make adaptations to the ones outlined. The important thing is, make sure you train regularly. If you do, then you will see an improvement in your fitness which, in turn, will mean an improvement in your game and that after all is what you are striving for – to become a better squash player. Remember one golden rule when training which applies whether you are ghosting, doing track runs, or weight training, and that is: No pain – no gain.

SQUASH

Simon Parke at the Singapore Open, 1989; the youngest player
ever to represent England.

SIX

INJURIES
PREVENTION & CURE

There are two types of injury the squash player is likely to suffer; trauma and overuse. It is essential that squash players know how to cope with these injuries, what to do when they occur, where to go for treatment, and better still, how to prevent the injuries from happening in the first place.

The top squash players spend hours on stretching routines which will help reduce the risk of injury when playing. The average club player can also prevent injury if he is sensible and takes the right precautions both before and during a match.

Warming up exercises:
Neck-stretching exercise.

PREVENTION

Warming up

The best way to reduce the risk of injury is to warm up well before a game, and to warm down after a game. The following warm-up exercises cover every major part of your body, from your head to your toes, which is used in a game of squash.

Neck Look over your right shoulder and hold the position for 10 seconds. Move your head to a central position and pause briefly before looking over your left shoulder, again holding position for 10 seconds. Repeat five times.

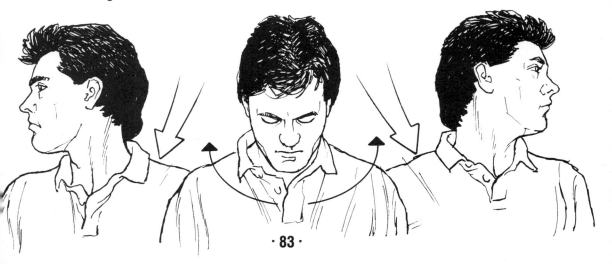

SQUASH

Wrist Hold both wrists in front of your chest and rotate 15 times, first clockwise, and then anti-clockwise.

Arms Hold both arms straight out behind your back and hold in position for 20 seconds. Another arm exercise is to hold your arms out in front of you and interlock your fingers. Keeping your arms straight, raise them above your head to full stretch and hold for 20 seconds.

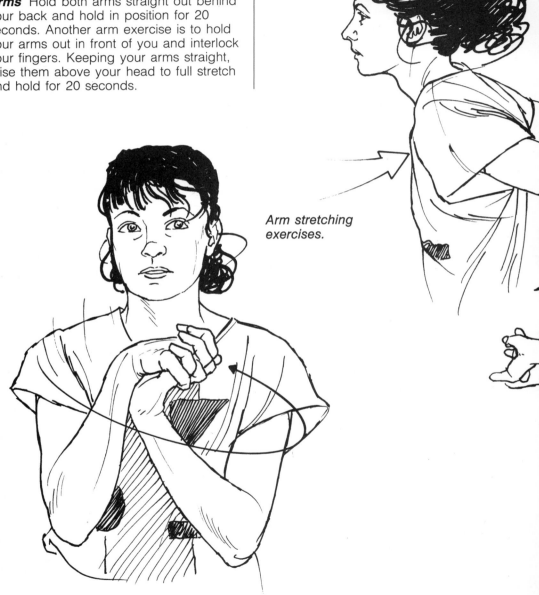

Arm stretching exercises.

Wrist mobility exercise.

SQUASH

Hips Put both hands on your hips and rotate the hips in a clockwise motion for 20 seconds. Repeat with the hips rotating in an anti-clockwise motion.

Hip mobility.

Shoulder exercise.

Shoulders Bring your right arm behind your back with the fingers facing upwards. Reach behind your neck with your left arm and grip your right hand. Hold the position for 20 seconds. Repeat the exercise with the arms reversed.

Trunk exercises.

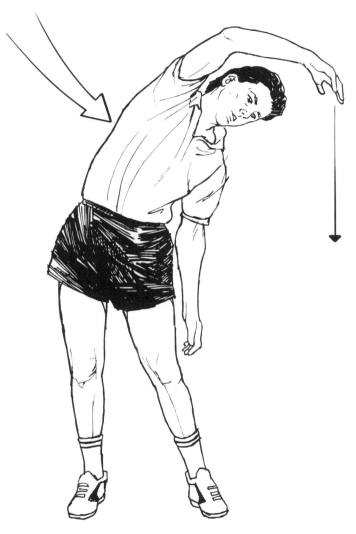

Trunk Stand with your legs apart and arms by your side. Bring your right arm over your head so the fingers point towards the floor. Stretch as far as possible and hold for 20 seconds. Repeat with the other arm.

SQUASH

Buttocks Sit on the floor and put your right foot over your left knee. Pull your left foot up to the right buttock. Put your forearm over your right knee and pull towards your left shoulder. Hold for 20 seconds and then repeat with your legs the opposite way around.

Legs (groin) Stand with legs apart and with your left foot pointing outwards. Keeping your left leg straight, bend the right knee. Keep your bottom above the level of your right knee. Don't lock the left knee. Hold in position for 20 seconds and then repeat with the right leg outstretched.

Buttocks exercise.

Leg stretching.

INJURIES – PREVENTION · AND · CURE

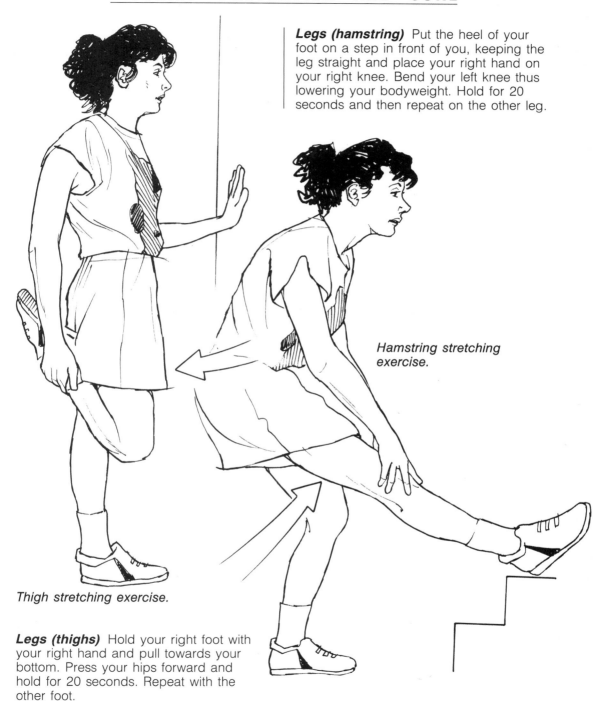

Legs (hamstring) Put the heel of your foot on a step in front of you, keeping the leg straight and place your right hand on your right knee. Bend your left knee thus lowering your bodyweight. Hold for 20 seconds and then repeat on the other leg.

Hamstring stretching exercise.

Thigh stretching exercise.

Legs (thighs) Hold your right foot with your right hand and pull towards your bottom. Press your hips forward and hold for 20 seconds. Repeat with the other foot.

Legs (calfs) Lean against a wall keeping your arms straight. Keep your left leg straight but bend the right knee. Put your weight onto your left foot by pressing your heel onto the floor. Hold for 20 seconds then repeat with the right leg outstretched.

Calf stretching exercise.

Legs (achilles tendons) Support your weight against a wall. Bend both knees and keep your heels flat on the floor. Hold for 20 seconds.

Ankles Stand with both feet apart. Lift the right foot slightly and rotate the heel in a clockwise direction 20 times and a further 20 times in an anti-clockwise direction. Repeat the exercise with the left foot.

After carrying out these exercises you should be sufficiently supple to start playing.

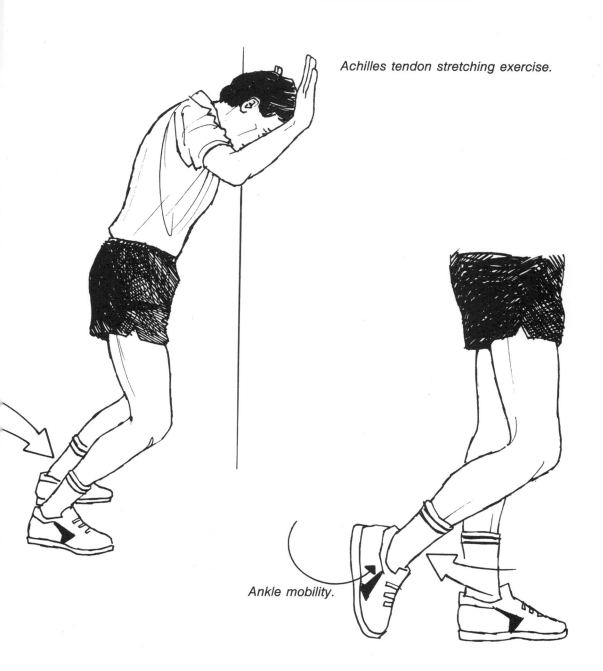

Achilles tendon stretching exercise.

Ankle mobility.

SQUASH

Rodney Martin of Australia. Notice his good balance, how the non playing hand is used as a counter-balance, and how Rodney never takes his eye off the ball.

Playing with the right equipment

A lot of squash injuries are caused because players don't have the right equipment. The two main tools of a squash player's 'trade' are his shoes and racket.

Shoes The majority of squash players do not wear the correct shoes. Instead they wear cheaper shoes with very little support, and these can cause all sorts of problems. When buying a pair of shoes you should consider the following points:

(a) Make sure the sole is made of rubber and has a good grip otherwise you could slip on sweat, which tends to gather on the floorboards.

(b) Make sure the inner sole has cushioning to support and take the shock of your foot striking the floor. You can buy separate shock absorbing heel pads or a whole unit to fit into the shoe.

(c) Make sure the upper part of the shoe does not retain your sweat. This part of the shoe needs to be made of mesh to enable your feet to breathe and thus prevent slippiness inside the shoe.

(d) Make sure the shoe is tight fitting to hold the feet firm. If the shoe is too big your foot will move in the shoe which will cause blisters.

(e) Perhaps the most important area of a shoe you should check when making your selection is the heel tab. If these are too high they will cause damage to your achilles tendons. You should either buy shoes with no heel tab or cut the tabs back. Heel tabs must not reach above the heel bone.

The racket The racket must be comfortable in your hand with the fingers spread comfortably around the grip. The grip must not be too thick, otherwise it will cause pressure on the muscles of your playing arm, which could give you cramps.

The racket itself must not be too heavy or too light. You need a well balanced racket with a little weight in the head to give control. The grip should either be of the towelling or cushioned type to absorb the sweat and make sure the racket doesn't slip in your hand. Leather grips tend to do this.

Eye protectors You can buy these from some sports goods shops. Many players, however, find them uncomfortable to play in, but if you can get used to them they will protect your eyes completely. A squash ball in the eye can be dangerous.

People who wear spectacles must ensure that the lenses are plastic. If they are made of glass they could shatter if hit by the squash ball and the result could be serious.

Clothing The clothing you wear must retain the perspiration. If it soaks through into your shirt and then drips onto the floor, a fall can result.

Shorts must not be too tight as this could restrict movement and cause injury due to a bad approach to a ball.

Wrist and head bands are also useful for absorbing sweat.

Injury can be caused by playing on the wrong type of court. Try to play on courts that have sprung floors as these take the pressure of impact caused by your leading leg striking the floor. Some courts are not sprung and this has the same effect as playing on concrete, which can cause knee problems.

Always make sure that the court is swept clean of dust and/or particles of rubber from the soles of shoes. If it is not swept you could slip and injure yourself. If a court floor has been sealed, be careful

because sweat does not soak into the floor and therefore creates a slippy court.

Injuries, of course, occur while you are playing. If you pull a muscle then you must stop playing at once otherwise you will aggravate the injury.

If you twist an ankle or knee the first thing you must do is put some ice on the injury for 20 minutes or so.

One of the more common squash injuries is being hit in the eye with the ball. If this happens you must seek proper medical advice so that the full extent of the injury can be assessed. It may appear 'nothing' at first sight, but only a trained medical person can make that decision.

To try to prevent the more common injuries while on court you should adhere to the following points:

(a) If your opponent is close to you while you are striking the ball, ask for a let (in some cases it would be your point). Do not try to hit the ball as you are likely to strike your opponent. It is better to be safe than sorry.

(b) Again, if your opponent is in the way stop and ask for a let. Don't try to run through at speed as this will probably cause your opponent to lose his balance, which in turn can cause injury.

When you have finished playing, always put your tracksuit on to keep your muscles and body warm. It is also important to warm down in a similar way as described in the section about stretching. The reason why you should warm down is to enable the lactic acid in your body to be drained out of your muscles instead of staying there, which would cause stiffness and cramps.

Jahangir Khan's balance is good, eyes watching the ball at all times. Notice that this drop shot is played when his opponent is out of position at the back of the court.

TYPES · OF · SQUASH · INJURIES

There are many injuries caused by playing squash. They are either caused by overuse of the joints, which means playing while slightly injured, or they are traumatic injuries. Over a period of time, an overuse injury will worsen and eventually stop you from playing.

A traumatic injury may occur while you are playing, *i.e.* twisted ankle, snapping an achilles tendon, or being hit by a racket which causes a cut. If any of these does occur then you must stop playing at once and receive the correct treatment. We will look more closely at the more common injuries the squash player will come across, and explain how to treat them.

Blistered feet

Blistered feet are usually caused by incorrectly fitted shoes or by playing a lot of matches. You must make sure that your shoes fit well and fit snugly to your feet. Wearing two pairs of socks helps restrict the movement of the foot within the shoe.

Hard skin often causes blood blisters which are very difficult to get rid of because you have to cut back the hard skin to 'pop' the blister. Always use a sterilized needle to stop infection. The best way to prevent these blisters is to rub the area of hard skin down with a scourer after each match, thus not letting the hard skin build up.

If you come off court with a blister that has burst and caused soreness then don't play again until is is better. But if blisters are a regular problem for you, seek the advice of a chemist or foot care specialist.

Bruised heels

Bruised heels are caused by the continuous pounding of your feet on the playing surface when hitting the ball. The only remedy for bruised heels is rest. It can take up to six weeks for the injury to remedy itself. Shock-absorbing heel cushions placed under the inner soles of your shoes will help reduce the risk of bruised heels. If the bruising is very close to the bone, which it often is, it can be very painful. Under no circumstances should you play again until the bruising has gone.

Achilles tendon

This injury is very traumatic if the tendon snaps. Normally, the tendon will feel a bit sore or inflamed. If that is the case, then ultra sound or laser treatment from a physiotherapist will help.

If the tendon snaps on court you will soon know about it. You will fall to the floor and be unable to stand. To check that it has snapped squeeze the calf. If the foot moves then you are lucky, it hasn't snapped.

Any player who snaps his tendon must immediately be taken to hospital for treatment. Recovery from this injury normally takes up to six months and it could even be a year before your are back on the squash court again. So, be patient.

Twisted ankle

This is one of the more common injuries which occur on the squash court. The ankle is normally twisted if you turn quickly and lose your balance, or can be caused by a slippy playing surface which causes you to 'go over' on your ankle. This can be extremely painful if you fall with your bodyweight on the ankle, and can damage the tendons.

The injury should be treated immediately by placing an ice pack on the ankle and wrapping it in a towel for at least 20 minutes. Keep your weight off the ankle. If you cannot apply pressure on the ankle after 20 minutes then you should go to hospital for an X-ray in case there is a cracked or broken bone. Treatment from a physiotherapist is recommended while you are recovering from this injury.

Calf muscles

This type of injury is generally not too traumatic, but still requires visits to the physio until the calf recovers. A bad calf strain can take up to six weeks to heal. Once you think you are ready to play squash again after a calf injury it is a good idea to go for a run on soft ground to see if the calf holds up under pressure.

SQUASH

The knee

Knee injuries fall into the category of those 'niggly' little injuries which many players don't take too seriously. Ideally, it is best to rest but many players think they can carry on playing. Do not try to play through pain because you will make the problem worse in the long term and create more serious problems. The message, again, is go and see a physio.

Some knee problems, such as those concerning the cartilage or patella (knee cap) require you to see a doctor for proper medical advice because surgery may be required. A basic weight lifting exercise may help to right the problem, but you must not consider such action until receiving confirmation from a doctor or specialist.

Thigh and hamstring

Thigh injuries are not all that common among squash players but are generally caused by overuse. During a game, the hamstring injury is more likely. If you pull a hamstring muscle, you must stop playing immediately, put ice on the problem area, and go to the physio. The hamstring injury is regarded as a serious one, and can keep you out of the game for anything up to eight weeks.

The back

Because of the bending and twisting required in a game of squash, the back is used more than any other part of your body. The twisting of the back is severe because you move at all sorts of angles very quickly as you react to reach the ball. This can cause overstretching which can in turn cause spasms or cramps in your back. Most back injuries start as a niggling pain before becoming extremely painful. If this is the case then, once more, you must stop playing immediately and seek advice from your doctor. Before you start playing again you should start with some other, gentler form of exercise like swimming or light work in the gym.

INJURIES – PREVENTION · AND · CURE

Arm and shoulder injuries

These are commonplace, especially to the playing arm. A sore wrist can happen because of poor technique, *i.e.* a floppy wrist which causes too much pressure on the tendons. The same applies to tennis elbow which, again, is caused through bad technique. You will be able to tell if you have tennis elbow because you will feel a pain in your elbow when holding the racket.

Shoulder problems tend to be less common among squash players. But when they do appear they normally start as a niggling irritation before developing into something more painful. Again, it is often the tendon area which is to blame.

These injuries involving the arms and shoulders should, once more, be taken to the physio who will administer the appropriate treatment.

Summing up

In all the above cases you should seek the advice from a qualified physiotherapist and whatever you do, don't play while suffering from an injury. You will only aggravate the situation.

HOW · TO · CURE · MOST · INJURIES

On the foregoing pages we have touched briefly on the cures for injuries. But we will now expand on those cures in more detail.

With those 'niggling' injuries, such as aching knees, a slight shoulder strain etc, you can carry on playing but you must undergo treatment at the same time so that the physio can keep an eye on the injury. The physio will use three basic forms of treatment:

(a) Ultra sound treatment.
(b) Laser treatment.
(c) Basic massage.

These treatments can cost more than £20 per session which, for some people will be considered costly, but it is better to be safe in the knowledge that your body is being properly looked after, rather than risk further, and possibly permanent damage.

Traumatic injuries must be treated straight away. As the injury will be very painful, you shouldn't need telling that you must stop playing immediately – your body will tell you!

We have mentioned several times that ice should be applied to the problem area. This keeps down the swelling and helps to stop any bruising.

After a traumatic injury, you should always go to hospital if the injury is serious; snapped achilles tendon, broken ankle, etc. After the initial medical treatment you will then be put on a course of physiotherapy and told not to play again until advised to do so by a specialist. Take, and listen to, this advice.

Like all sportsmen and women, squash players like to 'test' the injury before it is ready for the vigours of the sport after an injury. The advice is – don't.

Most squash injuries are caused by poor preparation by the player. Remember to warm up and prepare for your match. Don't go on to court cold and with stiff muscles.

It is useful to carry a small amount of first aid equipment around in your sports bag in readiness for the following minor injuries:

Cuts over the eye Carry butterfly plasters. Hold the cut together and administer the plaster. If the cut is too deep, however, you will have to go to hospital for professional treatment.

Blisters Make sure you have some big plasters in your bag. Apply an antiseptic spray before putting the plaster on the affected area.

Supports Also carry these for troubled areas such as ankles, knees, and elbows. Make sure the supports are reasonably tight otherwise they are of no use. But don't use ones that are so tight that they restrict the blood flow.

Chris Walker of England has good preparation for the forehand drop, the wrist is kept firm to control the ball and his opponent is behind him so that there is plenty of time to push the ball into the front corner.

CHILDREN · AND · INJURIES

When playing a sport like squash, children put a lot of pressure on their bodies. They must be closely monitored by their parents (or coach) as to how much physical pressure they can withstand. This doesn't necessarily apply to the boy or girl who plays the game just once a week; they won't be able to play to a high enough standard for the physical aspect of the game to be a problem.

The type of youngster we are talking about is the enthusiastic player who is playing in a tournament every weekend or is in a squadding system. Some of these children can be pushed too hard by over-zealous parents who have no idea about the game and don't understand its demands and possible ultimate consequences. The youngsters must want to play the game and not be pushed into it.

Squash is a tremendously physical sport and when a child is growing, his or her bones are soft which means they are prone to injury. If the parent or coach sees problems then the child must stop playing immediately and seek advice from a medical expert. A child should do little or no physical training until they are in their middle or late teens. Squash in itself is enough to keep a child fit.

One of Britain's outstanding prospects is the 18-year-old Simon Parke. He has been playing squash since he was nine and he has constantly been under the watchful eye of both his father and his coach. Simon is one of the world's top players and hasn't bothered with any other form of serious physical exercise, the squash was enough for him as a teenager. So, if it is good enough for one of the world's top stars then it is enough for other youngsters. If you are a parent, don't push your child too much. And if you are a budding child star don't allow yourself to be pushed too hard.

Let's now look at the areas where youngsters are prone to injury. The key areas are:

(a) ankles
(b) achilles tendons
(c) knees
(d) elbows
(e) shoulders.

To protect the ankles and achilles tendons a good quality shoe with a low cut heel tab, as already outlined, should be worn. The signs to look for, or better still, to discuss with a youngster, are whether he or she has tenderness in the achilles tendon. This can be diagnosed by squeezing the area to see if there is any pain. If this is the case, seek advice and make sure the youngster stops playing immediately.

The knees cause more problems to the youngster than any other part of the body. The problem will start as a dull ache before developing into severe pain. Youngsters in everyday life will carry on their normal activities without letting it worry them. So, if you are a parent, watch your child while he or she is playing squash. Are they dragging a leg or limping on court? If so, stop them from playing and seek advice.

The elbow also tends to cause children major problems, often because the racket is too big and heavy. Make sure the racket has a light head. If the child is only eight or nine when taking up squash, buy a junior racket for them. This type of racket will be in proportion to their body size. Shoulder injuries are also often caused by an excessively heavy racket.

As a parent, by all means be supportive of your child, but, remember, it is he or she out on court, not you.

SEVEN

PROFESSIONAL
STYLE

We are now going to analyze four of the world's leading squash players; Ross Norman, Simon Parke, Chris Dittmar, and Jahangir Khan. All four come from different countries and as we analyze each player it will become apparent that each has his own very individual style and characteristics. These differences are not just apparent in play on the court; they highlight their different attitudes towards training programmes, mental approach, attitudes away from the court, diet and drink, coping with travelling the world and, of course, their own individual personality.

You should, of course, try to develop your own style. But it does no harm to look at the professional style of the top players. It will give you an insight into what is expected of the leading squash players today.

Most of today's professionals started playing squash at a very early age. All would have had some form of coaching in their early years, whether it be from a parent, or other mentor such as a regular coach who they could rely upon to sort out technical problems and help with training schedules.

Because squash is an individual game and the squash player is on his own when he gets on to the court, you will find that squash professionals are very determined people. That is because their success or failure is solely down to them.

Unlike their snooker counterparts, squash players are not surrounded by managers. This is largely due to the fact that squash is not one of the big television sports and consequently does not attract multi-million pounds-worth of sponsorship. The television companies shun squash because they say the ball is too small to be picked up by the cameras. Because the squash professional does not have a

manager, he is responsible for making his own arrangements, and negotiating his own contracts whether it be with clothing or shoe manufacturers, or anyone else. But this area is one that holds him in good stead later in life. Who knows, after his playing days he could always become manager to a snooker player!

It is dedication which turns good club players into top class professionals and you will find that most leading players practise for four hours every day, unless they are playing competitively. A typical day for one of the top players would be; (a) stretching exercises, (b) practice on court in the morning, (c) lunch and a rest, (d) back on court for a rigorous work out, (e) fitness session, (f) shower.

It is interesting to note that professionals tend to group themselves in certain 'pockets' around the British Isles so that they have plenty of fellow professionals of similar standard to practice and train with regularly. This, in turn, is good for young, up and coming, players who will have access to the best players in the world to give them guidance and help.

The game of squash, like most other sports these days, is being dominated by the younger players such as Simon Parke and Peter Marshall who, as teenagers, are capable of taking on the best players in the world.

Problems of the professional squash player

Unlike the average club player, the professional squash player will always employ the services of a physiotherapist if

Susan Devoy shows good footwork getting down to a low ball with one hand on the floor to keep balance. The racket head comes under the ball to lift it to the back of the court.

he is injured. The physio will advise the professional on what exercises he should do in order to mitigate an injury. (Many club players will continue playing if injured, which would be disastrous for the pro.) The professional player will also seek advice from a professional medical person in order to get the injury cured as quickly as possible and thus get back to playing the same game he loves as quickly as possible.

Injuries are a problem which occasionally face the professional, but probably the biggest problem is the vast amount of travelling he has to endure in pursuit of his profession. When playing overseas tournaments one of the biggest headaches can be jet lag with time differences of up to twelve hours playing havoc with the body's clock. The seasoned professional counteracts this by arriving early for a tournament and thus getting used to the time change. Some players, however, have such a good mental approach that jet lag isn't a problem for them.

Boredom is another problem for the professional squash player when he is away from home playing in a tournament. Once he has finished a match he cannot make too many plans because, assuming he won his first game, he will have to look forward to his next game. Socializing is out. Rather, it is a question of relaxing and getting the mental attitude right for the next game.

Happily, squash is a friendly game, and most of the professionals get on well together. The professional circuit is relatively small in comparison to some other sports and this helps to generate that feeling of friendship.

All professional squash players are super fit. Squash is certainly one of a few sports where you will not make it to the top if you are not fit. The squash professional's motto when training is no pain – no gain. We have mentioned this slogan during the fitness chapter, but if you want to make the grade in the world of squash then you want to have it implanted in your mind now.

THE · PLAYING · STYLES

Right, it's now time to look closely at our four selected players. All four are highly motivated individuals and have given years of dedication to the sport. That dedication has been rewarded with a trophy cupboard full of silverware.

ROSS · NORMAN (New Zealand)

Type of player

Ross is a very, very determined person. His game is based on long gruelling rallies and taking the ball early on the volley to put his opponent under pressure. Athletically, Ross is superbly fit. His movement around the court has been likened to that of a greyhound. He rarely has one foot too far away from the 'T'-position which consequently keeps him in control of any rally. He keeps the ball straight thus giving his opponent very few options of playing a winning shot into the front two corners.

Tactically, he plays a safe game and doesn't take many chances unless his opponent is far enough out of position for the winning shot to be made. Ross utilizes the court to its fullest and can move the ball to any part, tiring out his opponent. It is when his opponent is tiring that Ross will step in and take a few more chances because his opponent finds the ball difficult to retrieve due to his own tiredness.

At his peak, Ross was probably the best athlete in the game and moved about the court with remarkable economy. What energy he did use up was always under control and used efficiently.

Best shots

Ross Norman's best shot is probably his backhand working boast. He hits the boast from around the service box with an unusually flat racket face, causing a slight top spin which makes the ball 'dig' or 'grip' the front wall on impact. This makes the ball fade away into the side wall quickly and forces his opponent into making a negative return; enabling Ross to attack.

Another of Ross' top strokes is again from around the service box, but on the forehand side. He has an excessive swing on the forehand which pushes opponents into the back of the court. He then plays a drop shot or boast to win the rally.

A lot of players feel Norman's swing is over-exaggerated in this area, thus gaining an unfair advantage. But referees don't share their view and he is not often penalized because of his swing.

The other stroke which wins Norman a lot of rallies, especially when his opponent has tired, is his backhand drop. He plays this shot in the simplest of manners, when his opponent is behind him. First he moves into the back of the court making his opponent move out of the way. He then drops the ball, with little pace, into the nick or side wall.

Coupled with the basic volley, these three shots form the basis of Norman's attacking game.

Training

Training is Ross Norman's biggest asset. If you watch Ross on court you will appreciate how supple he is; he can even do the splits! This has come about because of years of stretching exercises crucial to any top ranking squash player. Ross will do stretching exercises every morning, and after every training session.

Before a match he will stretch for half-an-hour, and for another half-an-hour after the match. By doing this he is making sure he is always ready to play and at the same time reducing the risk of injury.

Ross does most of his hard training on court using court sprints as described in our fitness chapter. He will do court sprints for between 45 and 60 minutes with a very short break in between each sprint. But he is not content with one session. He will repeat it later in the day. He has been training like this for years.

Mental approach

Like all top players, this is one of Ross' strong areas. His temperament is good and during a match he concentrates on his game and his opponent and doesn't let any outside influence upset him.

On court he is a very hards person and 'takes no prisoners'. He won't stand for any nonsense from other players on court and deals with them by giving them a cold hard stare.

In 1983, Norman severely damaged his left knee during a parachute jump (which was something of a stupid pursuit for one of the world's leading players). He was ranked No.8 in the world at the time. Despite being told he would never be able to play squash at the highest level again he ignored this advice and spent hours in the gym carrying out exercises in the hope of rebuilding his shattered knee. Eventually, after many months, he was fit again to play. The story typifies Norman's single-minded approach to the game.

When he returned he was fitter than ever and was mentally a lot stronger. In 1986, Ross Norman showed how determination and mental ability can turn you into a champion. After countless defeats at the hands of Jahangir Khan, the New Zealander beat Khan 3–1 to win the world title in Toulouse. Furthermore, it was Jahangir's first defeat in more than five-and-a-half years. Little wonder the man who survived a bad parachute landing is known as 'The Iron Man' by his fellow professionals.

Ross Norman's position is perfect for the a drive. The back foot is well placed giving a perfect base from which to control the drive to length.

SIMON · PARKE
(England)

Type of player

The reason Simon Parke finds himself among Britain's small coterie of world class professionals is because he is only 18 years of age and has been playing for the senior England team since the 1989 World Team Championships, when he became the youngest player ever to represent England.

Simon has been playing squash since he was nine years old. He has a good pedigree because he has been coached well and steered in the right direction from this early age. He won every junior title the game could offer.

His style of game is basically an all-court game and is efficient in all aspects. Simon's defensive play is extremely good due to tight racket work and athletic ability. He keeps the ball tight down both side walls, giving his opponent few options to attack the ball. Again, like most leading players, Simon is very disciplined and practises for four hours a day. For somebody so young, he has remarkable powers of concentration.

Now that he has become physically stronger, Simon is using the volley more and is capable of putting a lot of pressure on more senior players. Barring injuries, the future for Simon Parke is very bright and a world top ten ranking is almost a certainty for England's most promising player.

Best shots

Simon's best shots are generally made when his opponent is far enough out of position. He is not a naturally gifted shot player like Rodney Martin (the world No.4), but has average ability in this area.

His best 'killing' shot is his forehand from behind the service box, striking the ball short and either hitting the nick or fading low into the side wall. He hits this shot with a lot of slice so the ball 'dies' when it hits the floor.

Another area where he attacks well is on the backhand volley, taking the pace off the ball and fading it into the front backhand corner; either a winning shot or the reason for a weak return from his opponent.

Defence is one of his better qualities. When under pressure he returns the ball to tight areas and actually puts pressure back onto his opponent. His best shot in such a position is the straight lob down the walls which gives him time to recover to the 'T'-position.

Finally, he has a good forehand drop and fades the ball away along the side wall and into the nick. He plays this shot particularly well because he puts just the right amount of pace on the ball.

A study in concentration; Simon Parke at the T, appraising his own lob.

SQUASH

Training

Because he is still young, Simon has not put a great deal of effort into training. He is still growing and pushing himself too much at this stage of his career could bring about injury. Having said this, he is playing matches approximately five days a week, which itself is a good form of training.

He does practise hard with the ball, which helps to keep him disciplined. By the time he is 19 he will be engaged in the hard physical training schedules the game demands of its top players if they want to stay at the top.

Mental approach

For someone so young, Simon's mental approach is superb. He never argues with the referee or shouts when playing. His mind is entirely on the game and the job in hand – beating his opponent. When under pressure he composes himself by either taking time between points or putting as much oxygen into his lungs as possible to prepare for the next shot.

He will not go for silly shots at a crucial stage of a game. If the game is poised at, say, 5-all, he will fight to win the next two points and not give them away by making silly mistakes.

Some players try to pressurize Simon on court by either getting in his way or running into him. They use these tactics to try and intimidate him because of his age but it doesn't work. In fact, it has the opposite effect and spurs Simon on to play better.

Simon Parke is learning all the time and is Britain's best hope of producing a male world champion since the legendary Jonah Barrington.

He plays squash full-time and is managed by his father. He has no off-court distractions and this can only benefit his game. He is the most sought-after property in British squash and sponsors are clamouring be be associated with him. This is because of his age, his potential and his sportsmanship. If anybody can benefit from what sponsorship money the game of squash attracts, then Simon Parke is certainly one of those players. He has all the right credentials.

CHRIS · DITTMAR (Australia)

Type of player

Chris Dittmar is one of the most exciting players of the modern era. Chris has great deception qualities on court and his ability to finish a rally is second to none in the modern game.

At 6ft he is quite tall for a squash player, but he is very nimble around the court because he is always on his toes. Players find him difficult to read because he has a strong wrist. This means he can change the direction of the ball at the last minute and can therefore send his opponent the wrong way or put him under extreme pressure when attempting to retrieve the ball.

Chris also has the ability to take the ball very early on the volley which often has the effect of causing his opponent to stop before assessing where to go to cover the ball. This, of course, is a big advantage to Chris's game because it causes players to tire easily.

As he is so tall, it is hard to get the ball past him and put him into the back of the court. This means he often has a monopoly of the 'T'-position which enables him to play attacking squash to all four corners of the court.

He hits the ball extremely hard and with a short backswing, which is another facet of his deception. This aspect of squash is something that cannot be coached. It is a natural ability and Chris Dittmar has been blessed with his fair share of it.

Best shots

Chris has a great repertoire of shots from which to draw, but the ones that give him the greatest pleasure are those which send his opponent the wrong way. His deceptive cross-court drop shot works well from the front of the court. He holds the racket as long as possible before striking the ball, thus giving the impression he is going to play the straight drop. But a quick flick of the wrist sends the ball across court and thus wrongfoots his opponent.

Another of his favourite strokes is the straight arm drop shot. This shot is played about 2–3in (5–7.5cm) above the tin from the service box. The stroke must be close to the side wall, forcing a weak return. He then attacks the return to the back.

Chris also favours the forehand cross court nick on the volley. It is a shot he plays after forcing his opponent deep into the back of the court. He then volleys the ball with cut into the opposite corner, away from his opponent, rolling out of the nick and across the floor, giving his opponent no chance of retrieving the ball.

Chris uses every inch of the court to his advantage, especially the height on the front wall to give himself time to get into position and also to vary the pace on the ball. This often causes his opponent to snatch at the ball and hit a bad length, which Chris can then exploit.

Training

Chris has to train regularly to make sure he remains nimble and also to keep a check on his weight. Being so tall, he could easily put on excessive pounds. It is only in the last few years that he has trained seriously and regularly. But the benefits are very plain to see because he has risen to the top of the squash ladder in the last couple of years.

Like Ross Norman, it was an injury that made Chris decide that he had to train harder. Perhaps, like Norman, he realized how lucky he was to be given a second chance, so he worked harder at training.

He now spends most of his time practising short sprint movements, which

suits his type of game. Chris tends to attack the ball, which probably requires greater fitness than retrieving the ball.

Mental approach

Chris is very positive in his approach and like the majority of Australians is a tough competitor. He can, however, get a little upset if he believes opponents are calling for too many lets when they should be playing the ball.

However, you won't find him saying much or expressing himself on court because he is trying to maintain his concentration for each point. He just indicates in a professional manner his wish for his opponent to get on with the game.

Like most top players, Chris won't notice the crowd when playing because he creates his own coccoon and doesn't let noise from the crowd interfere with his concentration.

This position is perfect for Chris Dittmar's forehand drive. Notice the early racket preparation, and cocked wrist with the chest square to the side wall.

JAHANGIR · KHAN (Pakistan)

Type of player

Jahangir has everything in his game; he is probably the greatest player of all time. He has won every major title and went five-and-a-half years without defeat.

Jahangir tends to base his game on width and length. He is the most skilful of players, but only chooses to use his skills to the full when his opponent is far enough out of position for him to hit a winner. The reason for this is because length is his main principle. Jahangir does not go for too many shots because he is likely to make too many unforced errors or openings in the court, giving his opponent

Jahangir Khan is perfectly still at impact with perfect footwork and balance and the racket prepared with a cocked wrist at a 45-degree angle.

too many chances for playing winning shots.

His striking of the ball is ferocious, giving his opponent little time to react and putting him under immense pressure. Because of his strength, he can strike the ball like this constantly throughout a match, and rarely gets tired. He never gives his opponents time to settle on the ball and, therefore, they are never in the 'driving seat'. They are constantly on the defensive when playing Jahangir.

When playing into the front two corners he uses a lot of cut on the ball to keep it low and tight to the wall.

Best shots

There are few shots which Jahangir is not a master of. But his best shot is undoubtedly his back hand drop from just in front of the 'T'-area. His positioning is perfect and his opponent is kept deep by Jahangir pushing him back with his racket and body. He then delivers the drop which never misses.

Jahangir keeps the ball straight from the back of the court when hitting deep into the back corners. Also, he causes the ball to 'die' in the back corners putting a lot of pressure on the retriever.

The volleys he produces are extremely powerful which, again, keep his opponent in the back corners. This gives him time to choose when to play his volley drop as a winner.

When speaking to other players about Jahangir, they will say he has no weaknesses. The continuous pressure he applies wears opponents down to the point of frustration. One example of this was in the 1982 ISPA Tournament, when Jahangir played Magisood Ahmad of Pakistan, ranked No.3 in the world at the time. Jahangir won 9-0, 9-0, 9-0. Players ranked No.3 in the world don't lose by those sort of scores – unless they're playing Jahangir that is!

Training

It is reported that when Jahangir first made the breakthrough into the top flight of world squash he was training six hours a day on a programme that included swimming, sprints, ball exercises, and hard games. But the one thing which really helped his game was regularly playing good class players. This brought about a quick improvement.

Jahangir is capable of lasting out a $2^3/_4$-hour game if required (which he was called upon to do in the final of the 1983 Chichester Tournament against Gamal Awad). Needless to say Jahangir won. Awad was never the same player after this and rapidly slipped down the rankings.

In the mid-eighties, Jahangir Khan was fitter, mentally stronger, and more dedicated than any other man on the squash circuit. That is why he went five-and-a-half years without defeat.

Mental approach

Jahangir has always been disciplined mentally. He is an unassuming sort of person, is not arrogant, and will always speak to people. He leads a disciplined lifestyle and does not drink alcohol because of his religion.

Jahangir was motivated into doing well at squash following the death of his brother Torsum Khan who, tragically, died on court in Australia. He was a big influence on Jahangir as a youngster, and when Torsum died Jahangir set his sights on becoming a world champion one day, not only for himself but for his late brother. He has since fulfilled that ambition many times.

On court, Jahangir is the ultimate professional. He will never argue and rarely shows any signs of emotion which gives no clues to his opponent how he is feeling mentally or physically.

The world of squash will probably never see another player of Jahangir's quality. Happily he is still among the elite of the game and it will be interesting to see how long he can stay at the top.

Having analyzed four of the world's leading squash players you will probably have identified four features common to all of them:

(a) Dedication.
(b) Physical fitness.
(c) Mental toughness.
(d) Good ambassadors for the sport.

If you, as the good club player, can incorporate some, or all, of these qualities into your game then you are well on your way to improving your own game.

TESTING TIME

A series of question, and answers, to see how much you have learned on the foregoing pages.

1. What is the commonest mistake made by club players when playing the drive?
   (a) they take their eye off the ball
   (b) they adopt an incorrect balance
   (c) they move to the ball in a direct line

2. When playing either a straight or cross court drive where should you aim for the ball to land?
   (a) close to the back wall
   (b) close to the back of the service box
   (c) close to the front of the service box

3. When playing the drive with cut, what effect will the cut have?
   (a) It will cause the ball to bounce irregularly off the wall or floor or
   (b) It will cause the ball to 'die' more quickly in the corners after striking the side wall or floor

4. When lobbing what is the elementary mistake?
   (a) Not getting the ball high enough on the front wall
   (b) Poor timing
   (c) Incorrect stance

5. Which one of the following is a valid reason for using the lob as a tactical shot against a player who hits the ball hard?
   (a) It will tire your opponent out
   (b) Because it slows the pace of the game down

6. The skid and trickle are varieties of which shot?
   (a) lob
   (b) boast
   (c) drive

7. When playing the two- or three-wall boast, where, ideally, should the shot be played?
   (a) the 'T'
   (b) just behind the service box
   (c) close to the front wall

8. Which of the following are important when volleying?
   (a) balance
   (b) timing
   (c) correct swing

9. Approximately how many inches above the tin should the ball hit the front wall when playing the drop shot?
   (a) 2
   (b) 5
   (c) 10

10. What is the best position for playing the drop shot?
   (a) From the service box with your opponent behind you
   (b) From the 'T' with your opponent behind you
   (c) Anywhere when your opponent is adjacent to you, playing the ball to the opposite side of the front wall

11. Why shouldn't you play the drop shot too early in the rally?
   (a) It will let your opponent know you have it in your repertoire
   (b) It is not likely to be a point winning shot
   (c) It should be used later in the rally when your opponent is tiring

12. If you play a cross-court drop what should you always apply to the ball?
   (a) cut
   (b) sidespin
   (c) backspin

13. If you are the receiver at service what should you be concentrating on?
   (a) your opponent
   (b) the front wall
   (c) the ball

14. When employing the basic serve, how high above the service line should you aim the ball at the front wall?
   (a) 1ft
   (b) 2ft
   (c) 3ft

15. What is the most important shot for 'T' domination?
   (a) serve
   (b) volley
   (c) lob

16. What would you say is the prime objective in playing the ball, other than trying to win the rally?
   (a) moving your opponent off the 'T'
   (b) tiring your opponent out
   (c) gaining in confidence yourself

17. What is the most common error made when playing a straight drive from the back of the court?
   (a) trying to hit the ball too hard
   (b) trying to hit the ball with too much slice
   (c) trying to hit the ball too low

18. If your opponent is stuck in either of the back two corners of the court and is forced to play a boast, which is the best drop shot to play?
   (a) straight drop
      or
   (b) cross court drop

19. If your apponent is at the front of the court and you are on the 'T' which is the best shot to play?
   (a) cross court lob
   (b) three-wall boast
   (c) low hard volley

20. How would you describe the boast?
   (a) An attacking shot
      or
   (b) A defensive shot

SQUASH

ANSWERS

1. **(c)** move to the ball in a direct line
2. **(b)** close to the back of the service box
3. **(b)** It will cause the ball to 'die' more quickly in the corners after striking the side wall or floor
4. **(a)** Not getting the ball high enough on the front wall
5. **(b)** Because it slows the pace of the game down
6. **(b)** boast
7. **(b)** Just behind the service box
8. All three
9. **(a)** 2
10. **(b)** From the 'T' with your opponent behind you
11. **(c)** It should be used later in the rally when your opponent is tiring
12. **(a)** cut
13. **(c)** the ball
14. **(c)** 3ft
15. **(b)** volley
16. **(a)** moving your opponent off the 'T'
17. **(c)** trying to hit the ball too low
18. **(c)** straight drop
19. **(c)** low hard volley
20. **(a)** An attacking shot

Notice Susan Devoy's early preparation of the racket head for the volley, her good balance, and position to move to the 'T' as soon as the ball is struck.

GLOSSARY

Angle shot: A stroke played on to the side wall facing the striker before it reaches the front wall.

Back wall boast: A stroke played on to the back wall before it reaches the front wall.

Board or tin: The band, the top edge of which is .483 m (19 in) from the floor across the lower part of the front wall, above which the ball must be returned before the stroke is good.

Boast: The same as the angle shot, sometimes seen by players as a solely defensive stroke, which is a negative and unproductive approach (see page 24).

Check: A deliberate pause before playing a stroke in order to deceive an opponent.

Court sweating: Changes in temperature inside and outside of a court can cause moisture to form on the walls and floor. 'Sweating' makes the floor slippery and possibly dangerous and can cause the ball to skid on the walls.

Crowding: Restricting an opponent's movements by physical closeness to him.

Cut: Hitting the ball to give it backspin.

Cut line: A line on the front wall, the top edge of which is 1.829 m (6 ft) above the floor and extending the full width of the court.

Die: When the ball lacks sufficient momentum to bounce, so that it cannot be returned, it 'dies'.

Drop shot: A stroke played delicately on to the front wall so that it dies.

ESRF: European Squash Rackets Federation.

Footfault: Occurs if the server fails to stand with at least one foot inside the service box and does not touch the lines of the box at the moment of striking the ball.

Half-court line: A line on the floor of the court parallel to the side walls dividing the back half of the court into two equal parts.

Half-volley: A stroke played immediately after the ball has bounced, and on its rise.

Hammer service: A service hit very hard.

Hand: The period from the time a player becomes hand-in until he becomes hand-out.

Hand-in: The player who serves.

Hand-out: The player receiving service; also the term used to indicate that hand-in has become hand-out.

ISPA: International Squash Players Association.

ISRF: International Squash Rackets Federation – the governing body.

Kill: An unreturnable stroke.

Length: A stroke played so that the ball bounces only once before it hits the back wall and dies.

Mark: Each ball has a coloured mark denoting its speed: yellow, white, red, blue – slow to fast respectively.

Nick: The angle where the wall meets the floor. When the ball hits this angle and rolls across the floor it is dead.

GLOSSARY

Oak tree: The area in the centre of the court which the average player can reach whilst standing with one foot on the 'T'.

Quarter court: One part of the back half of the court which has been divided into two equal parts by the half-court line.

Screw service: When the ball bounces from the front wall on to the side wall nearest the server before reaching the receiver.

Set: When the score reaches 8 all, hand-out must choose before the next service is delivered, either to continue the game to 10, which is termed 'set two', when the player who first scores two more points wins the game, or declare 'no set' in which case the first player to reach 9 points wins the game.

Short line: A line set upon the floor parallel to and 5.48 m (18 ft) from the front wall and extending the full width of the court.

SRA: Squash Rackets Association – (British).

String: A racket may be strung with either natural gut or synthetic strings. Also, a string is the position of a player in a team, eg first string will be the number one player.

Stroke to: Term used by the referee when awarding the stroke to one of the players.

Veteran: Male player over 45 years of age (female over 40).

Vintage: Male player over 55 years of age.

WSRA: Women's Squash Rackets Association.

INDEX

Page references in **bold** refer to photographs.

INDEX

Also available in the Ward Lock
Ahead of the Game series:

GOLF by P.G.A. Captain Richard Bradbeer 07063 6884 3

TENNIS by L.T.A. Coach Anne Pankhurst 07063 6870 3

SOCCER by F.A. Coach Mike McGlynn 07063 6886 X